the Endeavour Journal of Joseph Banks

THE AUSTRALIAN JOURNEY

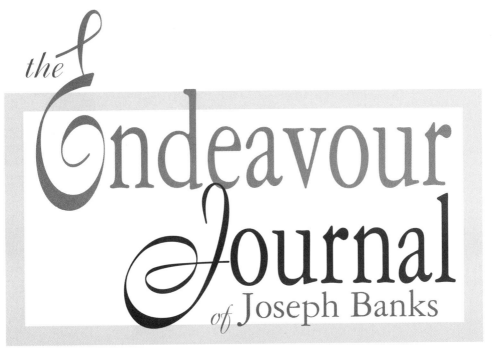

the Endeavour Journal of Joseph Banks

THE AUSTRALIAN JOURNEY

edited by

PAUL BRUNTON

 Angus&Robertson

An imprint of HarperCollins*Publishers*

in association with

STATE LIBRARY OF
NEW SOUTH WALES

Angus&Robertson
An imprint of HarperCollins*Publishers*, Australia
in association with
The State Library of New South Wales

First published in Australia in 1998
by HarperCollins*Publishers* Pty Limited
ACN 009 913 517
A member of the HarperCollins*Publishers* (Australia) Pty Limited Group
http://www.harpercollins.com.au

HarperCollins*Publishers*
25 Ryde Road, Pymble, Sydney NSW 2073, Australia
31 View Road, Glenfield, Auckland 10, New Zealand
77–85 Fulham Palace Road, London W6 8JB, United Kingdom
Hazelton Lanes, 55 Avenue Road, Suite 2900, Toronto, Ontario M5R 3L2
and 1995 Markham Road, Scarborough, Ontario M1B 5M8, Canada
10 East 53rd Street, New York NY 10032, USA

National Library of Australia Cataloguing-in-Publication data:

Banks, Joseph, Sir, 1743–1820.
    The Endeavour journal of Joseph Banks : the Australian
    journey.
    Bibliography.
    ISBN 0 207 19736 9.
    1. Endeavour (Ship). 2. Natural history - Australia. 3.
    Voyages around the world. 4. Australia - Discovery and
    exploration. I. State Library of New South Wales. II.
    Title.
919.4041

Designed and Produced by Maritime Heritage Press Pty Ltd
80A Queen Street, Woollahra NSW 2025
Designer: Lucy Dougherty
Cover: "A view of Endeavour River, on the coast of New Holland
where the ship was laid ashore to repair the damage she received on the
rock", in Sydney Parkinson, *A journal of a voyage to the South Seas*,
London, 1773. ML Q980/P.

Printed in Singapore by Kyodo Printing Co. on 115gsm Matt Art

9 8 7 6 5 4 3 2 1
01 00 99 98

Contents

Editor's Note

*T*he voyage of *Endeavour*, commanded by James Cook, from 1768 to 1771, inaugurated the history of European settlement in Australia.

Cook had been instructed to sail to Tahiti to observe the transit of the planet Venus across the face of the sun, an event that was predicted to occur on 3 June 1769. These observations would help scientists calculate the distance of the sun from the earth, providing a greater understanding of the extent of the solar system.

Cook was further instructed to search for the legendary southern continent. The west coast of New Zealand, discovered by Abel Tasman in the summer of 1642–43, was thought by some to be the west coast of a vast landmass. Cook demolished this supposition by circumnavigating New Zealand, proving it to be two islands and producing a map of remarkable accuracy.

He then turned west and sailed up the east coast of Australia — the first European to do so — naming it first 'New Wales' and then 'New South Wales' and taking possession of it in the name of King George III at an island he named 'Possession Island' off the tip of Cape York.

The voyage had been undertaken at the urging of the Royal Society, a distinguished assembly of those interested in all aspects of science. One of its Fellows was Sir Joseph Banks (1743–1820) — young, rich and passionate about natural history.

He had been elected in 1766, not owing to great scientific learning but because of his social connections. He had recently inherited his baronetcy, was now Sir Joseph, and had 5000 pounds a year at his disposal.

Young men of Banks' age and station were wont to make the Grand Tour of Europe — plundering its treasures, sampling its fleshpots, and picking up a little culture on the way, if only by error. Banks is alleged to have remarked of these diversions: 'Every blockhead does that; my Grand Tour shall be one around the whole globe.'

Precisely how he negotiated a passage on *Endeavour* for himself and his party of eight is not known. Much would have been discussed over the dinner table and no written record kept. The Royal Society formally recommended him to the Admiralty and Their Lordships agreed, no doubt influenced by the fact that Banks would pay for himself and his suite.

A contemporary described *Endeavour*'s voyage as 'the Argonautic Expedition for the Study of Nature', as indeed it was to be. Banks brought with him two naturalists, Daniel Carl Solander and Herman Deidrich Sporing, both Swedish in origin, to describe what would be found. The artists, Alexander Buchan and Sydney Parkinson, were included to draw what would be seen. Being a gentleman, Banks travelled with a number of personal assistants and servants: James Roberts and Peter Briscoe, who came from Banks' Lincolnshire estate; and Thomas Richmond and George Dorlton, both of whom were negroes: very exotic and very chic accessories for a rising young milord of the 1760s.

Banks brought a substantial library of over 100 volumes, preserving bottles, nets, hooks, trawls, devices for catching insects, a sort of underwater telescope, artists' materials, paper for drying and storing specimens — all the paraphernalia of the natural historian. He also took a guitar which he was skilled in playing, and his dogs — including greyhounds for chasing game. It was alleged that he spent 10 000 pounds on the voyage.

Endeavour's great cabin, by rights the captain's domain, was shared with Banks and his retinue, who used it as a work area. Banks was to write later:

> seldom was a gale so strong that it interrupted our usual time of study, which lasted from approximately 8 o'clock in the morning until 2 o'clock in the afternoon, and from 4 or 5 o'clock, when the smell of cooking had vanished, we sat together until it got dark at a big table in the cabin with our draughtsman directly opposite us and showed him the manner in which the drawing should be done and also hastily made descriptions of all the natural history subjects while they were still fresh. When a longer absence from land had exhausted the supply of fresh subjects we finished the former descriptions and added synonyms from the books that we carried along with us.

Endeavour sailed from Plymouth on Thursday 25 August 1768 with 94 people on board. Throughout the voyage, whenever it was calm, Banks and his assistants were out in a small boat, catching fish and plants in a net, or shooting birds. When the ship landed their first task was to go 'botanizing' on shore. Banks was always busy as his party set to work examining, sketching, and preserving: his excitement and wonder was evident from the first.

After calling at Madeira in September, they sailed down to Rio de Janeiro arriving in November. Here Banks compared himself with the mythical Tantalus, forever condemned to grasp at fruit which he could not reach, because the Viceroy of Brazil refused him permission to collect. He nonetheless had plants smuggled in with the food, and on one occasion Banks himself stole out under cover of darkness.

In January 1769, they reached Tierra del Fuego, the archipelago at the southern tip of South America, separated from the mainland by the Strait of Magellan. In freezing temperatures, Banks went ashore, and here his two servants, Richmond and Dorlton, having stolen a bottle of rum and consumed its contents, died in the snow.

Crossing the immense waters of the Pacific, they arrived at Tahiti in April 1769 where they remained for three months, occupied with preparations for observing the Transit. No land mass was seen en route, and Banks commented that many square miles of the southern continent beloved of the speculative writers had been changed into water, and their ideas liquefied.

Banks spent his time collecting, observing the local customs and enjoying the company, and the beds, of Tahitian women. He also, as he would do later in New Zealand and Australia, compiled accurate vocabularies of the local language.

At Tahiti, Tupaia, a nobleman originally from the island of Raiatea, joined the *Endeavour* with his servant as part of Banks' entourage. He was to prove useful in communicating with the Maoris when the ship reached New Zealand. Banks looked forward to keeping Tupaia 'as a curiosity, as well as some of my neighbours do lions and tygers', but Tupaia died before reaching England.

Having observed the Transit, the expedition left Tahiti in July 1769. Just before they reached the east coast of New Zealand, at Poverty Bay in October, Banks wrote a vivid description of his working life on board:

> now do I wish that our friends in England could by the assistance of some magical spying glass take a peep at our situation: Dr Solander setts at the Cabbin table describing, myself at my Bureau journalizing, between us hangs a large bunch of sea-weed, upon the table lays the wood and barnacles; they would see that notwithstanding our different occupations our lips move very often and without being conjurers might guess that we were talking about what we would see upon the land which there is no doubt we shall see very soon.

After *Endeavour* circumnavigated New Zealand, between October 1769 and March 1770, Banks reported the 'total demolition of our aerial fabrick called continent' as the great southern continent, the Terra Australis Incognita, seemed more and more a myth.

The condition of *Endeavour* made sailing back to South America in winter too hazardous and so the decision was made to seek the east coast of New Holland and the strait which was thought to exist between it and New Guinea.

Australia was first sighted on the 20th of April 1770 at Cape Everard, Victoria. From here *Endeavour* sailed up the east coast and eventually in August 1770 passed through Torres Strait by way of Endeavour Strait, between Prince of Wales Island and the mainland.

They arrived at Batavia (Jakarta) in October 1770. This was disastrous for their health and 30 of the crew died either here or on their way back to England, which the *Endeavour* reached in July 1771. Of Banks' original party of eight, only three survived: Richmond and Dorlton perished in South America; Buchan died of epilepsy at Tahiti; Parkinson and Sporing died of dysentery contracted at Batavia. Sailing around the world for three years was a risky business.

Banks returned with around 30 000 plant specimens, revealing 1400 species new to science, and about one thousand species of animal were collected. Drawings of nearly 1000 plants and 298 of animals had been made. Banks and Solander became the darlings of society; they were presented to the King, and awarded honorary doctorates by Oxford University.

From first to last Banks kept a journal — on loose sheets of paper and in a hand which had not yet been reduced by age and gout to illegibility. It is the foundation document of White Australia. It gives the first accurate and extensive description of the country, and the first of the east coast. It records Banks' initial engagement with the place which ever after, until his death in 1820, was inextricably linked with his name.

It was Banks who recommended Botany Bay to a House of Commons Committee in 1779 as a suitable place for a penal settlement. It was Banks who corresponded confidentially with the early governors and in the case of William Bligh, the fourth Governor, engineered his appointment and had his salary doubled. Banks also sent out collectors to the Colony, and arranged the voyage of Matthew Flinders in 1801–1803 to complete the mapping of Australia. Governments could fall, interest in Australia could wane, but Banks was always there, guiding and directing.

The journal Banks kept on the *Endeavour*, the Australian section of which is published here, is preserved in the Mitchell Library, State Library of New South Wales. It has had an eventful history from the time Banks wrote it and it is something of a miracle that it has survived intact.

It was lent to John Hawkesworth who compiled (with notable incompetence) the official account of the *Endeavour* voyage, published in 1773. It was later given to Matthew Flinders as a work of reference on his circumnavigation of Australia, and then returned to England in a trunk from Mauritius, where Flinders was imprisoned. It was handed around to a number of potential biographers of Banks following his death in 1820.

By the 1890s the journal was in the hands of Sir John Henniker Heaton, a member of the British parliament who had been to Australia. Because of his interest he was known as the 'Member for Australia'. In 1894 Heaton sold the journal to Alfred Lee of Sydney. Lee was a book collector, in competition with the doyen of Australian collectors and founder of the Mitchell Library, David Scott Mitchell. For years Mitchell pursued Lee for the journal, realising that his own collection would not be complete without it. Finally in 1906, Mitchell bought Lee's entire collection. One year later, on Mitchell's death, the journal formed part of his bequest to the nation.

Banks' journal was first published, after a fashion, in 1896. It was edited by Joseph Dalton, an outstanding botanist but a slipshod and delinquent editor: paragraphs and pages were omitted, and much of what remained was rewritten.

In 1962, the complete text was published for the first time by the State Library of New South Wales in association with Angus & Robertson Publishers, edited by John Cawte Beaglehole, the distinguished scholar of Cook's voyages. It is Beaglehole's transcription of the text that is reproduced in this edition.

The text of Banks' *Endeavour* journal reproduced here retains Banks' spelling and punctuation. Spaces in the text were left by Banks. He no doubt intended to add information later.

Some confusion has arisen over the correct dating of certain events, owing to the difference between ship's time and civil time. Time on board ship was calculated by the sun and the day began at midday, twelve hours prior to civil time which began at midnight. Cook's official logbook was kept in ship's time: Banks' journal in civil time. In addition, for those parts of the journal after the ship had crossed the 180th meridian of longitude (the future International Date Line), the date should be advanced one day to conform with today's calendar. For example, when Banks records the landing at Botany Bay under the 28th of April, it should be corrected to the 29th.

Paul Brunton
Curator of Manuscripts
State Library of New South Wales

1. *This engraving is from a portrait by Joshua Reynolds of a young Joseph Banks,
soon after his return, in 1774.*

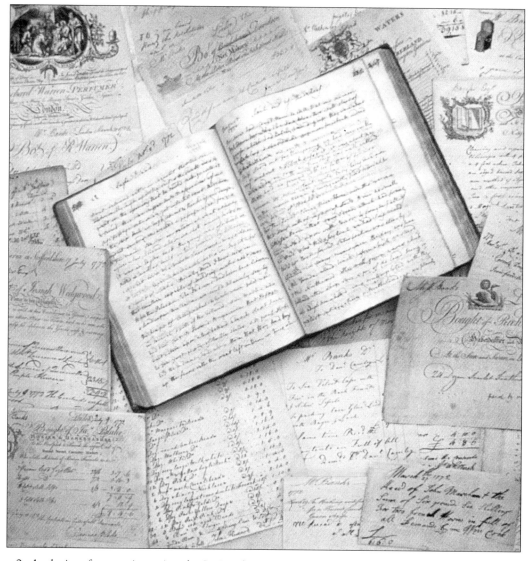

2. *A selection of manuscripts written by Sir Joseph Banks including (centre) the* Endeavour Journal, *in the Mitchell Library collection.*

The Journal

1st April – 26th August 1770

April 1770

With the first day light this morn the Land was seen ...

The Tasman Sea

1. William Brougham Monkhouse, died at Batavia (Jakarta) 5 November 1770.

2. 'wort' is an infusion of malt.

3. David MacBride, *Historical account of the new method of treating the scurvy*, 1768. It recommended an infusion of malt as a protection against scurvy.

APRIL 1. Fresh breeze and fair all day.

APRIL 2. Wind more to the westward but still fair. — Our malt having turnd out so indifferent that the Surgeon[1] made little use of it a method was thought of some weeks ago to bring it into use, which was to make as strong a wort[2] with it as possible and in this boil the wheat which is servd to the People for breakfast. It made a mess far from unpleasant which the people soon grew very fond of: myself who have for many months constantly breakfasted upon the same wheat as the people, either did or at least thought that I receivd great benefit from the use of this mess, it totaly banishd in me that troublesome Costiveness which I beleive most people are subject to when at sea. Whether or no this is a more beneficial method of administering wort as a preventative than the common must be left to the faculty, especialy that excellent surgeon Mr M'Bride whose ingenious treatise on the sea scurvy can never be enough commended.[3] For my own part I should be inclind to beleive that the salubrious qualities of the wort which arise from fermentation might in some degree at least be communicated to the wheat when thouroughly saturated with its particles, which would consequently acquire a virtue similar to that of fresh vegetables, the most powerfull resisters of Sea scurvy known.

Towards land

APRIL 3. Wind as yesterday: we got fast on to the Westward but the Compass shewd that the hearts of our people hanging that way caus'd a considerable North variation which was sensibly felt by our navigators, who calld it a current as they usualy do every thing which makes their reconings and observations disagree.

APRIL 4. Wind and weather precisely as yesterday.

APRIL 5. Wind is rather abated and weather considerably milder. The Captn told me that he has during this whole vo[y]age observd that between the degrees of 40° and 37° South latitude the Weather becomes suddenly milder in a very great degree, not only in the temperature of the air but in the Strenght and frequency of the gales of wind, which increase very much in going towards 40 and decrease in the same proportion as you aproach 37.

APRIL 6. Almost calm, the air very mild. Some dusky coulourd birds were seen by Tupia[4] and the Master[5] who both sayd they were of a sort which they had not seen before. Tupia also declard that he saw a flying fish, no one else however observd it.

4. Tupaia, a priest, was taken on board at Tahiti in April 1769 as part of Banks' retinue. He died at Batavia on 20 December 1770.

5. Robert Molyneux, 1746–1771.

APRIL 7. Almost calm: the air both yesterday and today was damp so that many things began to mould. The sun today had greater power and heat than we had felt for some months past.

APRIL 8. No swell today, Very light breezes, sun and air much as yesterday.

APRIL 9. Fair breeze tho very little of it: the Sea both yesterday and today was as smooth as a millpool, no kind of swell ranging in any direction. In the Morn a red taild Tropick bird was seen who hoverd some time over the ship but except him few or no Birds appeard.

APRIL 10. Another red taild tropick bird was seen today and a Flying fish. Weather as it has now been for several days rather troublesomly warm and the Sea most uncommonly smooth.

APRIL 11.   Calm: myself went out a shooting and killd *Diomedea exulans* and *impavida*, saw *profuga*; *Procellaria melanopus*, *Velox*, *Oceanica*, *Vagabunda* and *longipes*, *Nectris fuliginosa*,[6] which I find to be the same bird as was seen by the Master and Tupia on the 6th. Took up with dipping net *Mimus volutator*, *Medusa pelagica*, *Dagysa cornuta*, *Phyllodoce velella* and *Holothuria obtusata*, of which last an Albatross that I had shot dischar[ge]d a large quantity, incredible as it may appear that any animal should feed upon this blubber, whose stings innumerable give a much more Acute pain to a hand which touches them than Nettles.

APRIL 12. Calm again: I again went out in my small boat and shot much the same birds as yesterday; took up also cheifly the same animals to which was added indeed *Actinia natans*.[7] I again saw undoubted proofs that the Albatrosses eat Holothurias or *Portugese men of War* as the sea men call them. I had also an opportunity of observing the manner in which this animal stings. The body of it Consists of a bladder on the upper side of which is fixd a kind of Sail which he erects or depresses at pleasure; the edges of this he also at pleasure gathers in so as to make it Concave on one side and convex on the other, varying the concavity or convexity to which ever side he pleases for the conveniency of catching the wind, which moves him slowly upon the surface of the sea in any direction he pleases. Under the bladder hang down two kinds of strings, one smooth and transparent which are harmless, the other full of small round knobbs having much the appearance of small beads strung, these he contracts or extends sometimes to the lengh of 4 feet. Both these and the others are in this species of a lovely ultramarine blew, but in the more common one which is many times larger than this being near as large as a Gooses egg, they are of a fine red. With these latter however he does his mischeif, stinging or burning as it is calld if touchd by any substance: they immediately exsert millions of exceeding fine white threads about a line in lengh which peirce the skin and adhere to it giving very acute pain. When the animal exserts them out of any of the little knobbs or beads which are not in contact with some substance into which they can peirce they appear very visibly to the naked eye like small fibres of snow white cotton.

6. The first three are albatross; the next five are petrel and the last is probably a sooty shearwater.

7. A sea anemone.

APRIL 13. Calm and fine as Yesterday with the sun as powerfull as ever; last night a great dew fell with which in the morn all the rigging &c was wet. Myself shooting as usual but saw no new birds except a *Gannet* which came not near me: of those for these 4 or 5 days past killd a good many, indeed during this whole time they have been tame and appeard unknowing and unsupicious of men, the generality of them flying to the boat as soon as ever they saw it which is generaly the case when at large distances from the land. Took up *Dagysa vitrea* and *Gemma, Medusa radiata* and *Porpita, Helix Janthina* very large, *Doris complanata* and *Beroe biloba.* Saw a large shoal of *Esox Scombroides* leaping out of the water in a very extrordinary manner, pursued by a large fish which I saw but could not strike tho I did two of the former. In the Evening saw several fish much Resembling *Bonitos.*

The weather we have had for these Nine days past and the things we have seen upon the sea are so extrordinary that I cannot help recapitulating a little. The Weather in the first place which till the fifth was cool or rather cold became at once troublesomely hot bringing with it a mouldy dampness such as we have experiencd between the tropicks: the Thermometer at this time although it shewd a considerable difference in the degree of heat was not near so sensible of it as our bodies, which I beleive is generaly the case when a damp air accompanies warmth. During the continuance of this weather the inhabitants of the seas between the tropicks appeard: the Tropick bird, flying fish and *Medusa Porpita* are animals very seldom seen out of the influence of trade winds, several others also are such as I have never before seen in so high a latitude and never before in such perfection as now except between the tropicks. All these uncommon appearances I myself can find no other method of accounting for than the uncommon lengh of time that the wind had remain in the Eastern quarter before this, which Possibly had all that time blown home from the trade wind, and at the same time as it kept the sea in a quiet and still state had brought with it the Produce of the Climates from whence it came.

APRIL 14. A great dew this morn and Weather as calm as ever; in the afternoon however a small breeze sprang up and increasd gradualy till towards night when a large quantity of Porpoises were seen about the ship.

APRIL 15. Little or no Dew this morn: the Breeze freshned and came to WNW which soon raisd a sea. Several flying fish were seen today; tho I was not fortunate enough to see any of them yet they were seen by people who I am sure could not be mistaken. After dinner a small Bird of the *Sterna* kind came about the ship much like the Sterna [8] of New Zealand but browner upon the back; it stayd a long time about the ship and seemd to me as if it had lost its way. At night the wind moderated but with it came a kind of invisible spray or mist which thouroughly wetted my hair as I walkd the deck.

8. There follows a space in the manuscript where Banks no doubt intended to add later the scientific name.

9. Zachary Hicks, 1737–1771.

APRIL 16. No dew this morn: weather moderate and cloudy. In the Morn Tupia saw a large float of sea weed and shewd it to one other man; it was however so far from the ship that no one else saw it. At noon Our second Lieutenant[9] observd a small Butterfly as he thought. At night some Thunder and a fresh gale at SW, with a heavy swell which seemd to keep rather to the Westward of the Wind. Many Albatrosses and black shearwaters were about the ship. At night a small land bird came on board about the size of a sparrow; some of the boys tried to catch it but it got from them in the rigging and was never seen after.

APRIL 17. During last night and this morn the weather was most Variable with continual squalls and wind shifting all round the compass; such weather is often met with in the neighbourhood of land so that with this and the former signs our seamen began to prophesy that we were not now at any great distance from it. A Gannet was seen which flew towards the NW with a steady uninterrupted flight as if he knew the road that he was going led to the shore. In the evening a Port Egmont hen was seen. At night it blew strong at WSW.

APRIL 18. Stiff gales and a heavy sea from the Westward. In the morn a *Port Egmont hen* and a *Pintado bird* were seen, at noon two more of the former. At night the weather became rather more moderate and a shoal of Porpoises were about the Ship which leapd out of the water like Salmons, often throwing their whole bodies several feet high above the surface.

Cape Everard

10. The Australian coast was first sighted by Zachary Hicks at a place Cook named in Hicks' honour, Point Hicks. It was most probably present-day Cape Everard, Victoria.

11. One league is three miles, or about five kilometres.

APRIL 19. With the first day light this morn the Land was seen,[10] at 10 it was pretty plainly to be observd; it made in sloping hills, coverd in Part with trees or bushes, but interspersd with large tracts of sand. At Noon the land much the same. We were now sailing along shore 5 or 6 Leagues[11] from it, with a brisk breeze of wind and cloudy unsettled weather, when we were calld upon deck to see three water spouts, which at the same time made their appearance in different places but all between us and the land. Two which were very distant soon disapeard but the third which was about a League from us lasted full a quarter of an hour. It was a column which appeard to be of about the thickness of a mast or a midling tree, and reachd down from a smoak colourd cloud about two thirds of the way to the surface of the sea; under it the sea appeard to be much troubled for a considerable space and from the whole of that space arose a dark colourd thick mist which reachd to the bottom of the pipe. When it was at its greatest distance from the water the pipe itself was perfectly transparent and much resembled a tube of glass or a Column of water, if such a thing could be supposd to be suspended in the air; it very frequently contracted and dilated, lenghned and shortned itself and that by very quick motions; it very seldom remain in a perpendicular direction but Generaly inclind either one way or the other in a curve as a light body acted upon by wind is observd to do. During the whole time that it lasted smaler ones seemd to attempt to form in its neighbourhood; at last one did about as thick as a rope close by it and became longer than the old one which at that time was in its shortest state; upon this they Joind together ,in an instant and gradualy contracting into the Cloud disapeard.

APRIL 20. The countrey this morn rose in gentle sloping hills which had the appearance of the highest fertility, every hill seemd to be cloth'd with trees of no mean size; at noon a smoak was seen a little way inland and in the Evening several more.

APRIL 21. In the morn the land appeard much as it did yesterday but rather more hilly; in the even again it became flatter. Several smoaks were seen from whence we concluded it to be rather more populous; at night five fires.

Pigeon House Mountain

12. Cook called it the Pigeon House. It is near present day Ulladulla.

13. William Dampier, 1651–1715, published accounts of his landings in 1688 and 1699 on the western coast of Australia: *A new voyage round the world,* published in 1697 and *A voyage to New Holland,* published in two volumes 1703–1709. Both were very popular books and both gave disparaging views of the Australian Aborigines. The relevant extract from the 1697 publication is: 'the colour of their Skins, both of their Faces and the rest of their Body, is Coal-black, like that of the Negroes of Guinea'.

APRIL 22. The Countrey hilly but rising in gentle slopes and well wooded. A hill was in sight which much resembled those dove houses which are built four square with a small dome at the top.[12] In the morn we stood in with the land near enough to discern 5 people who appeard through our glasses to be enormously black: so far did the prejudices which we had built on Dampiers account[13] influence us that we fancied we could see their Colour when we could scarce distinguish whether or not they were men. — Since we have been on the coast we have not observd those large fires which we so frequently saw in the Islands and New Zealand made by the Natives in order to clear the ground for cultivation; we thence concluded not much in favour of our future freinds. — It has long been an observation among us that the air in this Southern hemisphere was much clearer than in our northern, these some days at least it has appeard remarkably so. A headland calld Dromedaries Head, not remarkably high, had been seen at the dist of 25 L'gs and judgd by nobody to be more than 6 or 8 from us; it was now in sight plain and our distance from it by the ships run was 23 l'gs, yet the Sea men acknowledg'd that tho they knew how far it was from them they could not think that it appeard more than 10 l'gs off. The hill like a pigeon house was also seen at a very great distance; the little dome on the top of it was first thought to be a rock standing up in the sea long before any other part was seen, and when we came up with it we found it to be several miles inland.

APRIL 23. Calm today, myself in small boat but saw few or no birds. Took with the dipping net *Cancer Erythroptamus, Medusa radiata, pelagica, Dagysa gemma, strumosa, cornuta, Holothuria obtusata, Phyllodoce Velella* and *Mimus volutator.* The ship was too far from the shore to see much of it; a larger fire was however seen than any we have seen before.

The Master today in conversation made a remark on the Variation of the Needle which struck me much, as to me it was new and appeard to throw much light on the Theory of that Phaenomenon. The Variation is here very small, he says: he has three times crossd the line of no variation and that at all those times as well as at this he has observd the Needle to be very unsteady, moving very easily and scarce at all fixing: this he shewd me: he also told me that in several places he has been in the land had a very remarkable effect upon the variation, as in the place we were now in: at 1 or 2 Leagues distant from the shore the variation was 2 degrees less than at 8 Lgs distance.[14]

14. The 'variation' is the difference between magnetic and true north, affected by the relative position of the magnetic pole, but also by smaller magnetic fields such as from metal on board ship, or from large land masses.

APRIL 24. The wind was unfavourable all day and the ship too far from the land for much to be seen; 2 large fires however were seen and several smaller. At night a little lightning to the Southward.

APRIL 25. Large fires were lighted this morn about 10 O'Clock, we supposd that the gentlemen ashore had a plentifull breakfast to prepare. The countrey tho in general well enough clothd appeard in some places bare; it resembled in my imagination the back of a lean Cow, coverd in general with long hair, but nevertheless where her scraggy hip bones have stuck out farther than they ought accidental rubbs and knocks have intirely bard them of their share of covering. In the even it was calm. All the fires were put out about 5 O'Clock. Several brown patches were seen in the sea looking much as if dirt had been thrown into it, but upon a nearer examination they provd to be myriads of small *dagysas*.

APRIL 26. Land today more barren in appearance that we hade before seen it: it consisted cheifly of Chalky cliffs something resembling those of old England; within these it was flat and might be no doubt as fertile. Fires were seen during the day the same as yesterday but none so large.

Off Bulli

APRIL 27. The Countrey today again made in slopes to the sea coverd with wood of a tolerable growth tho not so large as some we have seen. At noon we were very near it; one fire only was in sight. Some bodies of 3 feet long and half as broad floated very boyant past the ship; they were supposd to be cuttle bones which indeed they a good deal resembled but for their enormous size. After dinner the Captn proposd to hoist

out boats and attempt to land, which gave me no small
satisfaction; it was done accordingly but the Pinnace on being
lowerd down into the water was found so leaky that it was
impracticable to attempt it. Four men were at this time
observd walking briskly along the shore, two of which carried
on their shoulders a small canoe; they did not however attempt
to put her in the water so we soon lost all hopes of their
intending to come off to us, a thought with which we once
had flatterd ourselves. To see something of them however we
resolvd and the Yawl, a boat just capable of carrying the
Captn, Dr Solander, myself and 4 rowers was accordingly
prepard.[15] They sat on the rocks expecting us but when we
came within about a quarter of a mile they ran away hastily
into the countrey; they appeard to us as well as we could judge
at that distance exceedingly black. Near the place were four
small canoes which they left behind. The surf was too great to
permit us with a single boat and that so small to attempt to
land, so we were obligd to content ourselves with gazing from
the boat at the productions of nature which we so much wishd
to enjoy a nearer acquaintance with. The trees were not very
large and stood seperate from each other without the least
underwood; among them we could discern many cabbage
trees but nothing else which we could call by any name. In the
course of the night many fires were seen.

15. The *Endeavour* carried
three boats: the pinnace, the
yawl and the long boat. In
addition Banks had his own
'small boat'.

Botany Bay

APRIL 28. The land this morn appeard Cliffy and barren
without wood. An opening appearing like a harbour was seen
and we stood directly in for it. A small smoak arising from a
very barren place directed our glasses that way and we soon
saw about 10 people, who on our approach left the fire and
retird to a little emminence where they could conveniently see
the ship; soon after this two Canoes carrying 2 men each
landed on the beach under them, the men hauld up their boats
and went to their fellows upon the hill. Our boat which had
been sent ahead to sound now aproachd the place and they all
retird higher up on the hill; we saw however that at the beach
or landing place one man at least was hid among some rocks
who never that we could see left that place. Our boat
proceeded along shore and the Indians followd her at a
distance. When she came back the officer who was in her told
me that in a cove a little within the harbour they came down

to the beach and invited our people to land by many signs and word which he did not at all understand; all however were armd with long pikes and a wooden weapon made something like a short scymetar. During this time a few of the Indians who had not followd the boat remain on the rocks opposite the ship, threatning and menacing with their pikes and swords — two in particular who were painted with white, their faces seemingly only dusted over with it, their bodies painted with broad strokes drawn over their breasts and backs resembling much a soldiers cross belts, and their legs and thighs also with such like broad strokes drawn round them which imitated broad garters or bracelets. Each of these held in his hand a wooden weapon about 2½ feet long, in shape much resembling a scymeter; the blades of these lookd whitish and some though[t] shining insomuch that they were almost of opinion that they were made of some kind of metal, but myself thought they were no more than wood smeard over with the same white pigment with which they paint their bodies. These two seemd to talk earnestly together, at times brandishing their crooked weapons at us as in token of defiance. By noon we were within the mouth of the inlet which appeard to be very good. Under the South head of it were four small canoes; in each of these was one man who held in his hand a long pole with which he struck fish, venturing with his little imbarkation almost into the surf. These people seemd to be totaly engag'd in what they were about: the ship passd within a quarter of a mile of them and yet they scarce lifted their eyes from their employment; I was almost inclind to think that attentive to their business and deafned by the noise of the surf they neither saw nor heard her go past them. At 1 we came to an anchor abreast of a small village consisting of about 6 or 8 houses. Soon after this an old woman followd by three children came out of the wood; she carried several peice of stick and the children also had their little burthens; when she came to the houses 3 more younger children came out of one of them to meet her. She often looked at the ship but expressd neither surprize nor concern. Soon after this she lighted a fire and the four Canoes came in from fishing; the people landed, hauld up their boats and began to dress their dinner to all appearance totaly unmovd at us, tho we were within a little more than ½ a mile of them. Of all these people we had seen so distinctly through our glasses we had not been able to observe the least signs of Cloathing: myself to the best of my judgement plainly discernd that the woman did not copy our mother Eve even in the fig leaf.

After dinner the boats were mann'd and we set out from the ship intending to land at the place where we saw these people, hoping that as they regarded the ships coming in to the bay so little they would as little regard our landing. We were in this however mistaken, for as soon as we aproachd the rocks two of the men came down upon them, each armd with a lance of about 10 feet long and a short stick which he seemd to handle as if it was a machine to throw the lance. They calld to us very loud in a harsh sounding Language of which neither us or Tupia understood a word, shaking their lances and menacing, in all appearance resolvd to dispute our landing to the utmost tho they were but two and we 30 or 40 at least. In this manner we parleyd with them for about a quarter of an hour, they waving to us to be gone, we again signing that we wanted water and that we meant them no harm. They remaind resolute so a musquet was fird over them, the Effect of which was that the Youngest of the two dropd a bundle of lances on the rock at the instant in which he heard the report; he however snatchd them up again and both renewd their threats and opposition. A Musquet loaded with small shot was now fird at the Eldest of the two who was about 40 yards from the boat; it struck him on the legs but he minded it very little so another was immediately fird at him; on this he ran up to the house about 100 yards distant and soon returnd with a sheild. In the mean time we had landed on the rock. He immediately threw a lance at us and the young man another which fell among the thickest of us but hurt nobody; 2 more musquets with small shot were then fird at them on which the Eldest threw one more lance and then ran away as did the other. We went up to the houses, in one of which we found the children hid behind the sheild and a peice of bark in one of the houses. We were conscious from the distance the people had been from us when we fird that the shot could have done them no material harm; we therefore resolvd to leave the children on the spot without even opening their shelter. We therefore threw into the house to them some beads, ribbands, cloths &c.

as presents and went away. We however thought it no improper measure to take away with us all the lances which we could find about the houses, amounting in number to forty or fifty. They were of various lenghs, from 15 to 6 feet in lengh; both those which were thrown at us and all we found except one had 4 prongs headed with very sharp fish bones, which were besmeard with a greenish colour'd gum that at first gave me some suspicions of Poison. The people were blacker than any we have seen in the Voyage tho by no means negroes; their beards were thick and bushy and they seem'd to have a redundancy of hair upon those parts of the body where it commonly grows; the hair of their heads was bushy and thick but by no means wooley like that of a Negro; they were of a common size, lean and seem'd active and nimble; their voices were coarse and strong. Upon examining the lances we had taken from them we found that the very most of them had been us'd in striking fish, at least we concluded so from sea weed which was found stuck in among the four prongs. — Having taken the resolution before mention'd we return'd to the ship in order to get rid of our load of lances, and having done that went to that place at the mouth of the harbour where we had seen the people in the morn; here however we found nobody. — At night many moving lights were seen in different parts of the bay such as we had been us'd to see at the Islands; from hence we suppos'd that the people here strike fish in the same manner.

APRIL 29. The fires (fishing fires as we suppos'd) were seen during the greatest part of the night. In the morn we went ashore at the houses, but found not the least good effect from our present yesterday: No signs of people were to be seen; in the house in which the children were yesterday was left every individual thing which we had thrown to them; Dr Solander and myself went a little way into the woods and found many plants, but saw nothing like people. At noon all hands came on board to dinner. The Indians, about 12 in number, as soon as they saw our boat put off Came down to the houses. Close by these was our watering place at which stood our cask: they look'd at them but did not touch them, their business was merely to take away two of four boats which they had left at the houses; this they did, and haul the other two above high water mark, and then went away as they came. In the Evening 15 of them armd came towards our waterers; they sent two before the rest, our people did the same; they however did not wait for a meeting but gently retird. Our boat was about this time loaded so every body went off in her, and at the same time the Indians went away. Myself with the Captn &c were in a sandy cove on the Northern side of the harbour, where we hauld the seine and caught many very fine fish, more than all hands could Eat.

APRIL 30. Before day break this morn the Indians were at the houses abreast of the Ship: they were heard to shout much. At su[n]rise they were seen walking away along the beach; we saw them go into the woods where they lighted fires about a mile from us. Our people went ashore as usual, Dr Solander and myself into the woods. The grass cutters were farthest from the body of the people: towards them came 14 or 15 Indians having in their hands sticks that shone (sayd the Sergeant of marines[16]) like a musquet. The officer on seeing them gatherd his people together: the hay cutters coming to the main body appeard like a flight so the Indians pursued them, however but a very short way, for they never came nearer than just to shout to each other, maybe a furlong. At night they came again in the same manner and acted over again the same half pursuit. Myself in the Even landed on a small Island[17] on the Northern side of the bay to search for shells; in going I saw six Indians on the main who shouted to us but ran away into the woods before the boat was within half a mile of them, although she did not even go towards them.

16. John Edgcumbe.

17. Bare Island.

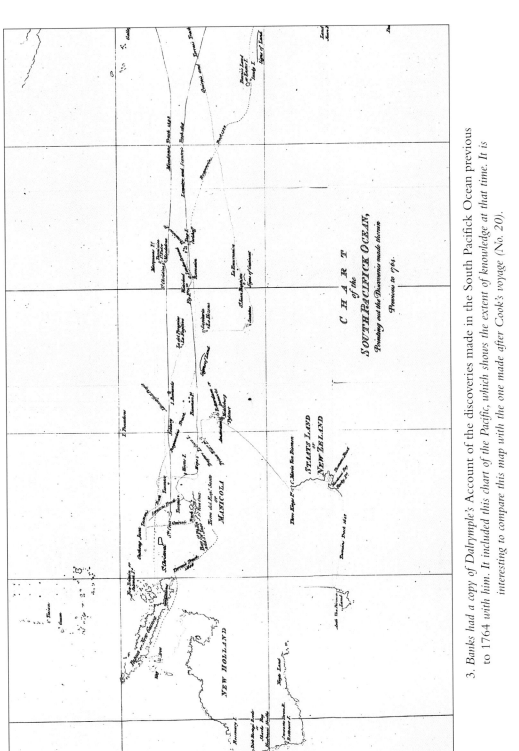

3. Banks had a copy of Dalrymple's *Account of the discoveries made in the South Pacifick Ocean previous to 1764 with him. It included this chart of the Pacific, which shows the extent of knowledge at that time. It is interesting to compare this map with the one made after Cook's voyage (No. 20).*

Flying Fish of St Jago. Cape De Verde Islands.
rather more than half the Size of Life. GT. 1791. Page 23.

4. *Banks developed as much of an interest in marine creatures such as flying fish as he did of land plants and animals, which is understandable given the amount of time he spent at sea.*

Portuguese Man of War (So called by Seamen). Its natural Size. GT. 1791. Page 41.

5. *In his journal under 12 April, Banks gives a detailed description of the 'Portugese men of War as the sea men call them', including his observations on their movement and stinging tentacles.*

May 1770

Myself in the woods botanizing as usual ...

Botany Bay

MAY 1. The Captn Dr Solander, myself and some of the people, making in all 10 musquets, resolvd to make an excursion into the countrey. We accordingly did so and walkd till we compleatly tird ourselves, which was in the evening, seeing by the way only one Indian who ran from us as soon as he saw us. The Soil wherever we saw it consisted of either swamps or light sandy soil on which grew very few species of trees, one which was large yeilding a gum much like *sanguis draconis*, but every place was coverd with vast quantities of grass. We saw many Indian houses and places where they had slept upon the grass without the least shelter; in these we left beads ribbands &c. We saw one quadruped about the size of a Rabbit, My Greyhound just got sight of him and instantly lamd himself against a stump which lay conceald in the long grass; we saw also the dung of a large animal that had fed on grass which much resembled that of a Stag; also the footsteps of an animal clawd like a dog or wolf and as large as the latter; and of a small animal whose feet were like those of a polecat or weesel. The trees over our heads abounded very much with Loryquets and Cocatoos of which we shot several; both these sorts flew in flocks of several scores together.

Our second Leutenant went in a boat drudging: after he had done he landed and sent the boat away, keeping with him a midshipman with whoom he set out in order to walk to the

Waterers. In his Way he was overtaken by 22 Indians who followd him often within 20 yards, parleying but never daring to attack him tho they were all armd with Lances. After they had joind our people 3 or 4 more curious perhaps than prudent, went again towards these Indians who remaind about ½ a mile from our watering place. When they came pretty near them they pretended to be afraid and ran from them; four of the Indians on this immediately threw their lances which went beyond our people, and by their account were thrown about 40 yards; on this they stoppd and began to collect the lances, on which the Indians retird slowly. At this time the Captn Dr Solander and myself came to the waterers; we went immediately towards the Indians; they went fast away, the Captn Dr Solander and Tupia went towards them and every one else stayd behind; this however did not stop the Indians who walkd leasurely away till our people were tird of following them. The accounts of every one who saw the Indians near today was exactly Consonant with what had been obsevd on the first day of our landing: they were black but not negroes, hairy, naked &c. just as we had seen them.

MAY 2. The morn was rainy and we who had got already so many plants were well contented to find an excuse for staying on board to examine them a little at least. In the afternoon however it cleard up and we returnd to our old occupation of collecting, in which we had our usual good success. Tupia who strayd from us in pursuit of Parrots, of which he shot several, told us on his return that he had seen nine Indians who ran from him as soon as they perceivd him.

MAY 3. Our collection of Plants was now grown so immensly large that it was necessary that some extrordinary care should be taken of them least they should spoil in the books. I therefore devoted this day to that business and carried all the drying paper, near 200 Quires of which the larger part was full, ashore and spreading them upon a sail in the sun kept them in this manner exposd the whole day, often turning them and sometimes turning the Quires in which were plants inside out. By this means they came on board at night in very good condition. During the time this was doing 11 Canoes, in each of which was one Indian, came towards us. We soon saw that the people in them were employd in striking fish; they came within about ½ a mile of us intent on their own employments and not at all regarding us. Opposite the place where they were several of our people were shooting; one Indian may be prompted by curiosity landed, hauld up his canoe and went towards them; he stayd about a quarter of an hour and then launchd his boat and went off, probably that time had been spent in watching behind trees to see what our people did. I could not find however that he was seen by any body. — When the damp of the Even made it necessary to send my Plants and books on board I made a small excursion in order to shoot any thing I could meet with and found a large quantity of Quails, much resembling our English ones, of which I might have killd as many almost as I pleasd had I given my time up to it, but my business was to kill variety and not too many individuals of any one species. — The Captn and Dr Solander employd the day in going in the pinnace into various parts of the harbour. They saw fires at several places and people who all ran away at their approach with the greatest precipitation, leaving behind the shell fish which they were cooking; of this our gentlemen took the advantage, eating what they found and leaving beads ribbands &c in return. They found also several trees which bore fruit of the Jambosa [18] kind, much in colour and shape resembling cherries; of these they eat plentifully and brought home also abundance, which we eat with much pleasure tho they had little to recommend them but a light acid.

MAY 4. Myself in the woods botanizing as usual, now quite void of fear as our neighbours have turnd out such rank cowards. One of our midshipmen stragling by himself a long way from any one else met by accident with a very old man and woman and some children: they were setting under a tree and neither party saw the other till they were close together. They shewd signs of fear but did not attempt to run away. He had nothing about him to give to them but some Parrots which he had shot: these they refusd, withdrawing themselves from his hand when he offerd them in token either of extreme fear or disgust. The people were very old and grey headed, the children young. The hair of the man was bushy about his head, his beard long and rough, the womans was crop'd short round

18. A space has been left in the manuscript where Banks no doubt intended to add later the scientific name.

her head; they were very dark colourd but not black nor was their hair wooley. He stayd however with them but a very short time, for seing many canoes fishing at a small distance he feard that the people in them might observe him and come ashore to the assistance of the old people, who in all probability belongd to them. 17 Canoes came fishing near our people in the same manner as yesterday only stayd rather longer, emboldend a little I suppose by having yesterday met with no kind of molestation. Myself in the afternoon ashore on the NW side of the bay, where we went a good way into the countrey which in this place is very sandy and resembles something our Moors in England, as no trees grow upon it but every thing is coverd with a thin brush of plants about as high as the knees. The hills are low and rise one above another a long way into the countrey by a very gradual ascent, appearing in every respect like those we were upon. While we were employd in this walk the people hawld the Seine upon a sandy beach and caught great plenty of small fish. On our return to the ship we found also that our 2nd lieutenant who had gone out striking had met with great success: he had observd that the large sting rays of which there are abundance in the bay[19] followd the flowing tide into very shallow water; he therefore took the opportunity of flood and struck several in not more than 2 or 3 feet water; one that was larger than the rest weigh'd when his gutts were taken out 239 pounds. Our surgeon, who had strayd a long way from the people with one man in his company, in coming out of a thicket observd 6 Indians standing about 50 yards from him; one of these gave a signal by a word pronouncd loud, on which a lance was thrown out of the wood at him which however came not very near him. The 6 Indians on seeing that it had not taken effect ran away in an instant, but on turning about towards the place from whence the lance came he saw a young lad, who undoubtedly had thrown it, come down from a tree where he had been Stationd probably for that purpose; he descended however and ran away so quick that it was impossible even to atempt to pursue him.

MAY 5. As tomorrow was fixd for our sailing Dr Solander and myself were employd the whole day in collecting specimens of as many things as we possibly could to be examind at sea. The day was calm and the Mosquetos of which we have always had

19. Cook first named the bay 'Sting Ray's Bay', later changing this to Botany Bay, in recognition of the great number of plants collected.

some more than usualy troublesome. No Indians were seen by any body during the whole day. The 2nd Lieutenant went out striking and took several large Stingrays the biggest of which weighd without his gutts 336 pounds.

20. They sailed past the entrance to Sydney Harbour, Cook naming it Port Jackson after George Jackson, Judge-Advocate at the Admiralty. Cook had worked as a stable boy on the estate of Jackson's sister at Ayton, Yorkshire.

MAY 6. Went to sea this morn with a fair breeze of wind. The land we saild past during the whole forenoon appeard broken and likely for harbours;[20] in the afternoon again woody and very pleasant. We dind to day upon the sting-ray and his tripe: the fish itself was not quite so good as a scate nor was it much inferior, the tripe every body thought excellent. We had with it a dish of the leaves of *tetragonia cornuta* boild, which eat as well as spinage or very near it.

MAY 7. During last night a very large dew fell which wetted all our sails as compleatly as if they had been dippd overboard; for several days past our dews have been uncommonly large. Most part of the day was calm, at night a foul wind.

MAY 8. Very light breezes and weather sultry all day. We had lost ground yesterday so the land was what we had seen before; upon it however we observd several fires upon it. At night a foul wind rose up much at the same time and much in the same manner as yesterday.

MAY 9. Wind continued foul and we turnd to windward all day to no manner of purpose.

21. i.e. the squall strained the rigging.

MAY 10. Last night a very heavy squall came off from the land which according to the seamens phrase made all sneer again;[21] it pay'd however for the trouble it gave by bringing a fair wind. In the morn the land appeard broken and likely for harbours; its face was very various, some parts being well wooded and others coverd with bare sand.

MAY 11. Fair wind continued. Land today trended rather more to the Northward than it had lately done, look'd broken and likely for inlets. At Sunset three remarkable hills were abreast the ship standing near the shore, of nearly equal size and shape; behind them the countrey rose in gradual slopes carrying a great shew of fertility.

22. Sydney Parkinson, part of Banks' entourage, natural history artist. He died 26 January 1771.

MAY 12. Land much as yesterday, fertile but varying its appearance a good deal, generaly however well clothd with good trees. This evening we finishd Drawing the plants got in the last harbour, which had been kept fresh till this time by means of tin chests and wet cloths. In 14 days just, one draughtsman[22] has made 94 sketch drawings, so quick a hand has he acquird by use.

MAY 13. Wind off shore today, it let us however come in with the land. Many porpoises were about the ship. At Noon several fires ashore, one very large which I judgd to be at least a league inland. Innumerable shoals of fish about the ship in the afternoon and some birds of the Nectris kind.

MAY 14. For these three nights last much lightning has been seen to the Eastward. Early in the morn it was calm and some few fish were caught; after the weather became squally. The wind however after some time settled at South, the briskest breeze I think that the Endeavour has gone before during the voyage. In the afternoon the land was rather more hilly than it has been. Several fires were seen and one high up on a hill side 6 or 7 miles at least from the beach.

MAY 15. Wind continued fair, a brisk breeze. The land in the Morning was high but before noon it became lower and was in general well wooded. Some people were seen, about 20, each of which carried upon his back a large bundle of something which we conjecturd to be palm leaves for covering their houses; we observd them with glasses for near an hour during which time they walkd upon the beach and then up a path over a gently sloping hill, behind which we lost sight of them. Not one was once observd to stop and look towards the ship; they pursued their way in all appearance intirely unmovd by the neighbourhood of so remarkable an object as a ship must necessarily be to people who have never

23. 60° Fahrenheit is 15.5° Celsius.

seen one. The Thermometer was at 60[23] which rather pinchd us. In the evening two small turtle were seen.

Mount Warning

At sun set a remarkable peakd hill was in sight 5 or 6 Leagues of in the countrey, which about it was well wooded and lookd beautifull as well as fertile. We were fortunate enough just at this time to descry breakers ahead laying in the very direction in which the ship saild; on this we went upon a wind and after making a sufficient offing brought too, but it blowing rather fresh and a great sea running made the night rather uncomfortable.

MAY 16. In the morn we were abreast of the hill and saw the breakers which we last night escapd between us and the land. It still blew fresh; at noon we were abreast of some very low land which lookd like an extensive plain in which we supposd there to be a Lagoon, in the neighbourhood of which were many fires.

MAY 17. Continued to blow tho not so fresh as yesterday. Land trended much to the westward; about 10 we were abreast of a large bay the bottom of which was out of sight.[24] The sea in this place suddenly changd from its usual transparency to a dirty clay colour, appearing much as if chargd with freshes, from whence I was led to conclude that the bottom of the bay might open into a large river. About it were many smoaks especialy on the Northern side near some remarkable conical hills. At sun set the land made in one bank over which nothing could be seen; it was very sandy and carried with it no signs of fertility.

MAY 18. Land this morn very sandy. We could see through our glasses that the sands which lay in great patches of many acres each were moveable: some of them had been lately movd, for trees which stood up in the middle of them were quite green, others of a longer standing had many stumps sticking out of them which had been trees killd by the sand heaping about their roots. Few fires were seen. Two water snakes swam by the ship; they were in all respects like land snakes and beautifully spotted except that they had broad flat tails which probably serve them instead of fins in swimming. In the evening I went out in the small boat but saw few birds of three sorts, Men of War birds (*Pelecanus aquilus*) Bobies (*Pelicanus Sula*) and *Nectris munda*, of which last shot one, and took up 2 cuttle bones differing from the European ones in nothing but the having a small sharp peg or prickle at one end.

24. Cook named this Morton Bay after the Earl of Morton. It appeared as 'Moreton' in the official published account of Cook's voyage and ever since. What Cook discovered was not present-day Moreton Bay but rather the bay formed by the coasts of Moreton and Stradbroke Islands behind which is Moreton Bay. Morton was President of the Royal Society from 1764 until his death a few weeks after *Endeavour* sailed. He never suffered the ignominy of his name forever misspelt.

Fraser Island

25. Fraser Island, though it was thought to be part of the mainland. Later named after Captain James Fraser who landed on the island in 1836 following the loss of his ship, *Stirling Castle.*

Hervey Bay

26. Hervey Bay, named by Cook after his friend Captain Augustus John Hervey, later an admiral and 3rd Earl of Bristol.

27. One fathom is six feet, or about 1.8 metres.

MAY 19. Countrey as sandy and barren as ever. Two snakes were seen, a man of war bird, and a small Turtle. At sun set the land appeard in a low bank to the sea over which nothing was seen, so that we imagind it was very narrow and that some deep bay on the other side ran behind it.[25]

MAY 20. At day break the land in sight terminated in a sandy cape behind which a deep bay[26] ran in, across which we could not see; our usual good fortune now again assisted us, for we discoverd breakers which we had certainly ran upon had the ship in the night saild 2 or 3 leagues farther than she did. This shoal extended a long way out from the land for we ran along it till 2 O'Clock and then passed over the tail of it in seven fathom[27] water; the Sea was so clear that we could distinctly see the bottom and indeed when it was 12 and 14 fathom deep the colour of the sand might be seen from the mast head at a large distance. While we were upon the shoal innumerable large fish, Sharks, Dolphins &c. and one large Turtle were seen; A grampus of the middle size Leapd with his whole body out of water several times making a Splash and foam in the sea as if a mountain had fallen into it. At sun set a few Bobies flew past towards the NW.

MAY 21. Land seen only from the mast head. Innumerable bobies for near 2 hours before and after Sun rise flew by the ship comeing from NNW and flying SSE, I suppose from some bird Island in that direction where they roosted last night. At 9 new land was in sight the other side of the bay which we left last night; as we aproachd it the depth of water gradualy decreasd to 9 fathom. At 4 in the evening the land appeard very low but coverd with fine wood; on it were many very large Smoaks several of which were seen before we could see the land itself. At night water still shoal, land low and well wooded, fertile to appearance as any thing we have seen upon this coast. At 8 came to an anchor till morn.

Bustard Bay

MAY 22. In the course of the night the tide rose very considerably. In the morn we got under sail again. The land as last night fertile and well wooded; at noon the land appeard much less fertile, near the beach it was sandy and we plainly saw with our glasses that it was coverd with Palm nut trees,

Pandanus Tectorius which we had not seen since we left the Islands within the tropicks. Along shore we saw 2 men walking along who took no kind of notice of us. At night we were working into a bay in which seemd to be good anchorage, where we came to an anchor resolvd to go ashore tomorrow and examine a little the produce of the countrey.

MAY 23. Wind blew fresh off the land so cold that our cloaks were very necessary in going ashore; as the ship lay a good way from the land we were some time before we got there; when landed however the sun recoverd its influence and made it sufficiently hot, in the afternoon almost intolerably so. We landed near the mouth of a large lagoon which ran a good way into the countrey and sent out a strong tide; here we found a great variety of Plants, several however the same as those we ourselves had before seen in the Islands between the tropicks and others known to be natives of the east Indies, a sure mark that we were upon the point of leaving the Southern temperate Zone and for the future we must expect to meet with plants &c. a part of which at least have been before seen by Europaeans. The Soil in general was very sandy and dry: tho it producd a large variety of Plants yet it never was coverd with a thick verdure. Fresh water we saw none, but several swamps and boggs of salt water; in these and upon the sides of the lagoon grew many Mangrove trees in the branches of which were many nests of Ants, one sort of which were quite green. These when the branches were disturbd came out in large numbers and revengd themselves very sufficiently upon their disturbers, biting sharper than any I have felt in Europe. The Mangroves had also another trap which most of us fell into, a small kind of Caterpiler, green and beset with many hairs: these sat upon the leaves many together rangd by the side of each other like soldiers drawn up, 20 or 30 perhaps upon one leaf; if these wrathfull militia were touchd but ever so gently they did not fail to make the person offending them sensible of their anger, every hair in them stinging much as nettles do but with a more acute tho less lasting smart. Upon the sides of the hills were many of the trees yeilding a gum like *Sanguis draconis*: they differd however from those seen in the last harbour in having their leaves longer and hanging down like those of the weeping willow, tho notwithstanding that I beleive that they were of the same species. There was however much less gum upon them; only one tree that I saw had any upon it, contrary to all theory, which teaches that the hotter a climate is the more gums exsude. The same observation however held good in the plant yeilding the Yellow gum, of which tho we saw vast numbers we did not see any that shewd signs of gum.

On the shoals and sand banks near the shore of the bay were many large birds far larger than swans which we judg'd to be Pelicans, but they were so shy that we could not get within gunshot of them. On the shore were many birds, one species of Bustard, of which we shot a single bird as large as a good Turkey. The sea seemd to abound in fish but unfortunately at the first hawl we tore our seine to peices; on the mud banks under the mangrove trees were innumerable Oysters, Hammer oysters and many more sorts among which were a large proportion of small Pearl oysters. Whither the sea in deeper water might abound with as great a proportion of full grown ones we had not an opportunity to examine, but if it did a pearl fishery here must turn out to immence advantage.

Those who stayd on board the ship saw about 20 of the natives, who came down abreast of the ship and stood upon the beach for some time looking at her, after which they went into the woods; we on shore saw none. Many large fires were made at a distance from us where probably the people were. One small one was in our neighbourhood, to this we went; it was burning when we came to it, but the people were gone; near it was left several vessels of bark which we conceivd were intended for water buckets, several shells and fish bones, the remainder I suppose of their last meal. Near the fires, for their were 6 or 7 small ones, were as many peices of soft bark of about the lengh and breadth of a man: these we supposd to be their beds: on the windward side of the fires was a small shade about a foot high made of bark likewise. The whole was in a thicket of close trees, defended by them from the wind; whether it was realy or not the place of their abode we can only guess. We saw no signs of a house or any thing like the ruins of an old one, and from the ground being much trod we concluded that they had for some time remain in that place.

MAY 24. At day break we went to sea. The weather was fine; we however were too far from the land to distinguish any thing but that there were some fires upon it tho not many. At Dinner we eat the Bustard we had shot yesterday, it turnd out an excellent bird, far the best we all agreed that we have eat since we left England, and as it weighd 15 pounds our Dinner was not only good but plentyfull. In the evening it drop'd calm and we caught some fish tho not many,

MAY 25. Land in the morn rocky, varied here and there with reddish sand, but little wood was to be seen. In the evening it was calm, some few fish were caught. At night perceiving the tide to run very strong we anchord. No fires were seen the whole day.

We examind the orange juice and brandy which had been sent on board as prepard by Dr Hulmes directions: See his letter p.   [28] It had never been movd from the cag in which it came on board. About ½ of it had been usd or leakd out; the remainder was coverd with a whitish mother but otherwise was not at all damagd either to taste or sight when it came out of the cag, but when put into a bottle in 3 or 4 days it became ropey and good for nothing. On this we resolvd to have it evaperated immediately to a strong essence and put up in Bottles immediately.

28. Banks left a space for the reference to a letter he had received prior to the voyage from Dr Nathaniel Hulme, regarding the treatment of scurvy.

Keppel Bay

29. They were between Great Keppel Island and the mainland. Cook named Keppel Bay, to the south, after Augustus Keppel, later First Lord of the Admiralty.

MAY 26. Standing into a channel with land on both sides of us and water very shoal, many rocky Islets, the main land very rocky and barren; at 1 the Water became so shallow that we came to an anchor.[29] While the ships boats were employd in sounding round about her myself in my small boat went a shooting and killd several bobies and a kind of white bird calld by the seamen Egg bird, *Sterna* .... Before I went out we tried in the cabbin to fish with hook and line but the water was too shoal (3 fhm) for any fish. This want was however in some degree [supplied] by Crabs of which vast numbers were on the ground who readily took our baits, and sometimes held them so fast with their claws that they sufferd themselves to be hawld into the ship. They were of 2 sorts, *Cancer pelagicus* Linn. and another much like the former but not so beautifull. The first was ornamented with the finest ultramarine blew conceivable with which all his claws and every Joint was deeply tingd; the under part of him was a lovely white, shining as if glazd and perfectly resembling the white of old China; the other had a little of the ultramarine on his Joints and toes and on his back 3 very remarkable brown spots. 2 fires were seen upon an Island, and those who went to sound in the boats saw people upon an Island also who calld to them and seemd very desirous that they should land. — In examining a fig which we had found at our last going ashore we found in the fruit of it a Cynips, very like if not exactly the same species with the *Cynips sycomori* Linn. describd by Haselquist in his *Iter Palestinum*;[30] a strong proof of the fact that figgs must be impregnated by means of insects, tho indeed that fact wanted not any additional proofs.

30. Fredrik Hasselquist's journal of his trip to Palestine and Egypt in 1749–52 was published in 1757.

MAY 27. The boats who sounded yesterday having brought back word that there was no passage ahead of the Ship we were obligd to return, which we did and soon fell in with the main land again which was barren to appearance; on it were some smoaks. We passd by many Islands. In the Eve the breeze was stronger than usual with Cloudy weather.

MAY 28. This morn at day break the water appeard much discolourd as if we had Passd by some place where a river ran into the sea; the land itself was high and abounded with hills. Soon after we came round a point into a bay in which were a multitude of Islands. We stood into the middle of them, a boat was sent a head to sound and made a signal for a shoal, on which the ship came too but before the anchor went she had less than 3 fathm water; the boats now sounded all round her and found that she was upon the shoalest part, on which the anchor was got up and we stood on. Weather was hazey; at night anchord.

Thirsty Sound

31. Thirsty Sound was so named by Cook because they could not find any fresh water.

MAY 29. Early this morn we got up our anchor and stood in for an opening in which by nine O'Clock we came to an anchor.[31] We saw in coming in no signs of People. After breakfast we went ashore and found several Plants which we had not before seen; among them were however still more East Indian plants than in the last harbour. One kind of Grass which we had also seen there was very troublesome to us: its sharp seeds were bearded backwards and whenever they stuck into our cloths were by these beards pushd forward till they got into the flesh: this grass was so plentifull that it was hardly possible to avoid it and with the Musketos that were likewise innumerable made walking almost intolerable. We were not however to be repulsd but proceeded into the countrey. The gum trees were like those in the last bay both in leaf and producing a very small proportion of Gum; on the branches of them and other trees were large ants nests made of Clay as big as a bushel, something like to those describd in Sr Hans Sloanes Hist of Jamaica[32] Voll. II, p. 221, t. 258, but not so smooth: the ants also were small and had whitish abdomens. In another species of tree *Xanthoxiloides mite*, a small sort of black ants had bord all the twigs and livd in quantities in the hollow part where the pith should be, the tree nevertheless flourishing, bearing leaves and flowers upon those very branches as freely and well as upon others that were sound. Insects in general were plentifull, Butterflies especialy: of one sort of these much like *P. Similis* Linn. the air was for the space of 3 or 4 acres crowded with them to a wonderfull degree: the eye could not be turnd in any direction without seeing milions and yet every branch and twig was almost coverd with those that sat still: of these we took as many as we chose, knocking them down with our caps or any thing that came to hand. On the leaves of the gum tree we found a Pupa or Chrysalis which shone almost all over as bright as if it had been silverd over with the most burnishd silver and perfectly resembled silver; it was brought on board and the next day came out into a butterfly of a velvet black changeable to blue, his wings both upper and under markd near the edges with many light brimstone colourd spots, those of his under wings being indented deeply at each end. We saw no fresh water but several swamps of salt overgrown with mangroves; in these we found some species of shells, Among them the *Trochus perspectivus* Linn. Here was also a very singular Phaenomenon in a small fish of   [33] of which there were great abundance. It was about the size of a minnow in England and had two breast finns very strong. We often found him in places quite dry where may be he had been left by the tide: upon seeing us he immediately fled from us leaping as nimbly as a frog by the help of his breast finns: nor did he seem to prefer

32. Hans Sloane *Voyage to the islands ... Jamaica, with the natural history ... of the last*, 1707–1725.

33. Space left by Banks in the manuscript. Dr J.C. Beaglehole in his 1962 edition of the journal comments: "The MS has a later pencil addition in this blank, the first word of which seems to be 'Globius'. This was a Mud-skipper or Walking Goby, and Banks' accurate observations on its habits seem to be the first to have been made. There are two genera and both occur in Australian waters."

water to land for if seen in the water he often leapd out and proceeded upon dry land, and where the water was filld with small stones standing above its surface would leap from stone to stone rather than go into the water: in this manner I observd several pass over puddles of water and proceed on the other side leaping as before. In the afternoon we went ashore on the opposite side of the bay: the productions were much like those on the side we were on in the morn, but if any thing the Soil was rather better. In neither morning nor evening were there any traces of inhabitants ever having been where we were, except that here and there trees had been burnt down.

MAY 30. Went again ashore in the same place as yesterday. In attempting to penetrate farther into the countrey it was necessary to pass a swamp coverd with mangrove trees; this we attempted chearfully tho the mud under them was midleg deep, yet before we had got half way over we heartily [repented of] our undertaking: so entangled were the archd branches of those trees that we were continualy stooping and often slipping off from their slimey roots on which we steppd; we resolvd however not to retreat and in about an hour accomplishd our walk of about ¼ of a mile. Beyond this we found a place where had been 4 small fires; near them were fish bones, shells &c. that had there been roasted, and grass layd together upon which 4 or 5 people had slept as I guessd about a fortnight before. Several of our people were ashore on liberty, one of these saw a small pool of standing water which he judgd to contain about a ton. Our second lieutenant saw also a little laying in the bottom of a gully near which were the tracks of a large animal of the Deer or Guanicoe kind; he who has been in Port Desire on the Coast of South America seemd to incline to think them like the latter. Some Bustards were also seen but none of them shot; Great Plenty however of the Beautifull Loriquets seen in the last but one anchoring place were seen and killd. The 2nd Lieutenant and one more man who were in very different places Declard that they heard the voices of Indians near them, but neither saw the People. The countrey in general appeard barren and very sandy; most of the trees were gum trees but they seemd not inclind to Yeild their gum, I saw only one tree which did. It was most destitute of fresh water, probably that was the reason why so few inhabitants were seen: it seemd to be subject to a severe rainy season, so at least we judgd by the deep gullys which we saw had been plainly washd down from hills of a small hight.

Whether the sea was more fruitfull than the land We had not an opportunity to try. It did not seem to promise much as we with our hooks and lines could catch nothing, nor were there any quantity of Oysters upon the shore. The tide rose very much, how high was not measurd, but I think I may venture to guess not less at spring tides than 18 or twenty feet, perhaps much more.

The Captn and Dr Solander went today to examine the bottom of the inlet which appeard to go very far inland; they found it to increase in its width the farther they went into it, and concluded from that and some other circumstances that it was a channel which went through to the sea again. They saw two men who followd the boat along shore a good way but the tide running briskly in their favour they did not chuse to stop for them; at a distance from them far up the inlet they saw a large smoak. At night they returnd and having found neither fresh water nor any other refreshment it was resolvd to leave this place tomorrow morn.

Bedwell Islands

MAY 31. Went out this morn, the weather misty and rainy and fresh breeze. As we had found by experience that many sands and shoals lay off the coast a boat was sent ahead; at noon she made a signal for shoal water on which we came to an anchor; the boats sounded and found a Passage on which we proceeded and at night came to an anchor under the shelter of an Island in the midst of Innumerable Islands, rocks and shoals.

6. *Chart of Botany Bay, published in John Hawkesworth:* An Account of the Voyages undertaken by Order of His Present Majesty for making Discoveries in the Southern Hemisphere, 1773.

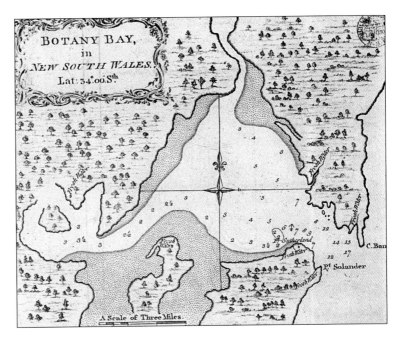

7. *The banksia is perhaps the best known of Banks' legacies to botany. This is* Banksia Serrata, *from the* Florilegium.

8. Acacia, *or* wattle, *from the* Florilegium.

9. *Sydney Parkinson was employed as a draughtsman by Banks. He died of dysentery in Batavia in January 1771. This portrait of him appeared in the publication of his own journal from the voyage, in 1773.*

June 1770

... scarce were we warm in our beds when we were call'd up with the alarming news of the ship being fast ashore upon a rock ...

Bedwell Islands

JUNE 1. In the night it raind and at times blew strong not much to our satisfaction who were in a situation not very desirable, as if our anchor should come home or cable break we had nothing to expect but going ashore on some one or other of the shoals which lay round us. The night passd however without the least accident, and at day light in the morn the anchor was got up and we proceeded, in hopes of getting out of our Archipelago. By noon we got in with the main land, which made hilly and barren; on it were some smoaks. In the Evening the weather settled fine and we saild along shore; at night came to an Anchor.

34. A symptom of scurvy.

Tupia complaind this evening of swelld Gums;[34] he had it seems had his mouth sore for near a fortnight, but not knowing what cause it proceeded from did not complain. The Surgeon immediately put him upon taking extract of Lemons in all his drink.

Cumberland Islands

JUNE 2. Sailing along shore with fine weather, the countrey hilly and ill wooded. Some Islands were still in sight ahead of us; at noon the irregularity of the soundings made it necessary to send the boat ahead again. In the evening the countrey was moderately hilly and seemd green and pleasant; one smoak was seen upon it. At night we anchord, several large Islands being without us.

Repulse Bay

35. Repulse Bay, named by Cook because he could not find a sheltered inlet in which to careen *Endeavour*.

36. Whitsunday Passage, named after the day on which it was discovered.

JUNE 3. At day break the anchor was weighd and we stood along shore till we found ourselves in a bay[35] off the outermost point of which were the Islands seen yesterday; by 8 it was resolvd to stand out again through a passage which was seen between them and the main[36] which was accordingly done. The countrey within the bay, especialy on the innermost side, was well wooded, lookd fertile and pleasant. After dinner standing among Islands which were very barren, rising high and steep from the sea; on one of these we saw with our glasses 2 men a woman and a small canoe fitted with an outrigger, which made us hope that the people were something improvd as their boat was far preferable to the bark Canoes of Stingrays bay.

Cape Upstart

37. The cape was so named by Cook because 'being surrounded with low land, it starts or riseth up singley at the first making of it'.

JUNE 4. Hills in the morn were high and steep[37] but they soon fell into very low land to all appearance barren. The water began now to be discolourd and an appearance of Islands was seen ahead which made us look out for more sholes. At noon one smoak was seen behind some hills inland. At night we passd pretty near a head land which appeard miserably rocky and barren. Much sea weed with very fine leaves passd by the ship all day.

JUNE 5. Land near the sea very low and flat behind which the hills rose: in the countrey very little appearance of fertility however either on one or the other: at noon one large fire was seen. Several Cuttle bones and 2 Sea Snakes swam past the ship. In the Even the Thermometer was at 74 and the air felt to us hotter than we have felt it on the coast before. Many Clouds of a thin scum lay floating upon the water the same as we have before seen off Rio de Janiero; some few flying fish also.

Magnetic Island

38. Cabo da Roca, north–west of Lisbon, Portugal: this 'cape' was actually Magnetic Island, named for its effect on the compass.

JUNE 6. Land made in Barren rocky capes; one in Particular which we were abreast of in the morn appeard much like Cape Roxent;[38] at noon 3 fires upon it. Many Cuttle bones, Some sea weed and 2 or 3 Sea snakes were seen. In the evening it fell quite calm and I went out in the small Boat and shot *nectris nugax* but saw nothing remarkable on the water; the weather most sultry hot in an open boat.

Palm Islands

JUNE 7. Sailing between the main and Islands, the main rose steep from the Water rocky and barren. Just about sun rise a shoal of fish about the size of and much like flounders but perfectly white went by the ship. At noon the Islands had mended their appearance and people were seen upon them; the Main as barren as ever with several fires upon it, one vastly large. After dinner an appearance very much like Cocoa nut trees tempted us to hoist out a boat and go ashore, where we found our supposd Cocoanut trees to be no more than bad Cabbage trees. The Countrey about them was very stoney and barren and it was almost dark when we got ashore; we made a shift however to gather 14 or 15 new plants after which we repaird to our boats, but scarce were they put off from the shore when an Indian came very near it and shouted to us very loud; it was so dark that we could not see him, we however turnd towards the shore by way of seeing what he wanted with us, but he I suppose ran away or hid himself immediately for we could not get a sight of him.

JUNE 8. Still sailing between the Main and Islands; the former rocky and high lookd rather less barren than usual and by the number of fires seemd to be better peopled. In the morn we passd within ¼ of a mile of a small Islet or rock[39] on which we saw with our glasses about 30 men women and children standing all together and looking attentively at us, the first people we have seen shew any signs of curiosity at the sight of the ship.

39. One of the Family Islands.

Cape Grafton

JUNE 9. Countrey much the same as it was, hills near the sea high, lookd at a distance not unlike Mores or heaths in England but when you came nearer them were coverd with small trees; some few flatts and valleys lookd tolerably fertile. At noon a fire and some people were seen. After dinner came to an Anchor and went ashore,[40] but saw no people. The countrey was hilly and very stony affording nothing but fresh water, at least that we found, except a few Plants that we had not before met with. At night our people caught a few small fish with their hooks and lines.

40. Mission Bay, near Cairns.

Green Island

JUNE 10. Just without us as we lay at an anchor was a small sandy Island laying upon a large Coral shoal, much resembling the low Islands to the eastward of us but the first of the kind we had met with in this part of the South Sea. Early in the

Cape Tribulation

morn we weighd and saild as usual with a fine breeze along shore, the Countrey hilly and stoney. At night fall rocks and sholes were seen ahead, on which the ship was put upon a wind off shore. While we were at supper she went over a bank of 7 or 8 fathom water which she came upon very suddenly; this we concluded to be the tail of the Sholes we had seen at sunset and therefore went to bed in perfect security, but scarce were we warm in our beds when we were calld up with the alarming news of the ship being fast ashore upon a rock, which she in a few moments convincd us of by beating very violently against the rocks. Our situation became now greatly alarming: we had stood off shore 3 hours and a half with a pleasant breeze so knew we could not be very near it: we were little less than certain that we were upon sunken coral rocks, the most dreadfull of all others on account of their sharp points and grinding quality which cut through a ships bottom almost immediately. The officers however behavd with inimitable coolness void of all hurry and confusion; a boat was got out in which the master went and after sounding round the ship found that she had ran over a rock and consequently had Shole water all round her. All this time she continued to beat very much so that we could hardly keep our legs upon the Quarter deck; by the light of the moon we could see her sheathing boards &c. floating thick round her; about 12 her false keel came away.[41]

41. The false keel was a protective strip attached below the actual keel.

JUNE 11. In the mean time all kind of Preparations were making for carrying out anchors, but by reason of the time it took to hoist out boats &c. the tide ebbd so much that we found it impossible to attempt to get her off till next high water, if she would hold together so long; and we now found to add to our misfortune that we had got ashore nearly at the top of high water and as night tides generaly rise higher than day ones we had little hopes of getting off even then. For our Comfort however the ship as the tide ebbd settled to the rocks and did not beat near so much as she had done; a rock however under her starboard bow kept grating her bottom making a noise very plainly to be heard in the fore store rooms; this we doubted not would make a hole in her bottom, we only hopd that it might not let in more water than we could clear with our pumps.

In this situation day broke upon us and showd us the land about 8 Leagues off as we judgd; nearer than that was no Island or place on which we could set foot. It however brought with it a decrease of wind and soon after that a flat calm, the most fortunate circumstance that could Possibly attend people in our circumstances. The tide we found had falln 2 feet and still continued to fall; Anchors were however got out and laid ready for heaving as soon as the tide should rise but to our great surprize we could not observe it to rise in the least.

Orders were now given for lightning the ship which was began by starting our water and pumping it up; the ballast was then got up and thrown over board, as well as 6 of our guns (all that we had upon deck). All this time the Seamen workd with surprizing chearfullness and alacrity; no grumbling or growling was to be heard throughout the ship, no not even an oath (tho the ship in general was as well furnishd with them as most in his majesties service). About one the water was faln so low that the Pinnace touchd ground as he lay under the ships bows ready to take in an anchor,[42] after this the tide began to rise and as it rose the ship workd violently upon the rocks so that by 2 she began to make water and increasd very fast. At night the tide almost floated her but she made water so fast that three pumps hard workd could but just keep her clear and the 4th absolutely refusd to deliver a drop of water. Now in my own opinion I intirely gave up the ship and packing up what I thought I might save prepard myself for the worst.

The most critical part of our distress now aproachd: the ship was almost afloat and every thing ready to get her into deep water but she leakd so fast that with all our pumps we could just keep her free: if (as was probable) she should make more water when hauld off she must sink and we well knew that our boats were not capable of carrying us all ashore, so that some, probably the most of us, must be drownd: a better fate maybe than those would have who should get ashore without arms to defend themselves from the Indians or provide themselves with food, on a countrey where we had not the least reason to hope for subsistance had they even every convenence to take

42. The first part of the 'heaving' operation was to load an anchor in the pinnace, row it some way away, and drop it to a secure hold on the seabed.

it as netts &c, so barren had we always found it; and had they even met with good usage from the natives and food to support them, debarrd from a hope of ever again seing their native countrey or conversing with any but the most uncivilizd savages perhaps in the world.

The dreadfull time now aproachd and the anziety in every bodys countenance was visible enough: the Capstan and Windlace were mannd and they began to heave:[43] fear of Death now stard us in the face; hopes we had none but of being able to keep the ship afloat till we could run her ashore on some part of the main where out of her materials we might build a vessel large enough to carry us to the East Indies. At 10 O'Clock she floated and was in a few minutes hawld into deep water where to our great satisfaction she made no more water than she had done, which was indeed full as much as we could manage tho no one there was in the ship but who willingly exerted his utmost strength.

JUNE 12. The people who had been 24 hours at exceeding hard work now began to flag; myself unusd to labour was much fatigued and had laid down to take a little rest, was awakd about 12 with the alarming news of the ships having gaind so much upon the Pumps that she had four feet water in her hold: add to this that the wind blew off the land a regular land breeze so that all hopes of running her ashore were totaly cut off. This however acted upon every body like a charm: rest was no more thought of but the pumps went with unwearied vigour till the water was all out which was done in a much shorter time than was expected, and upon examination it was found that she never had half so much water in her as was thought, the Carpenter[44] having made a mistake in sounding the pumps.

We now began again to have some hopes and to talk of getting the ship into some harbour as we could spare hands from the pumps to get up our anchors; one Bower[45] however we cut away but got the other and three small anchors far more valuable to us than the Bowers, as we were obligd immediately to warp her to windward that we might take advantage of the sea breeze to run in shore.

43. Heaving part two: the anchor line is wound in using the capstan, dragging the ship towards the secured anchor; the windlass was also needed owing to the number of anchors they had out.

44. John Satterley, died February 1771.

45. An anchor from the bow.

46. Jonathan Monkhouse, brother of the surgeon, died February 1771.

47. Loose fibrous material, used for caulking ships.

One of our midshipmen[46] now proposd an expedient which no one else in the ship had seen practisd, tho all had heard of it by the name of fothering a ship, by the means of which he said he had come home from America in a ship which made more water than we did; nay so sure was the master of that ship of his expedient that he took her out of harbour knowing how much water she made and trusting intirely to it. He was immediately set to work with 4 or 5 assistants to prepare his fother which he did thus. He took a lower studding sail and having mixd together a large quantity of Oakum[47] chopd fine and wool he stickd it down upon the sail as loosely as possible in small bundles each about as big as his fist, these were rangd in rows 3 or 4 inches from each other: this was to be sunk under the ship and the theory of it was this, where ever the leak was must be a great suction which would probably catch hold of one or other of these lumps of Oakum and wool and drawing it in either partly or intirely stop up the hole. While this work was going on the water rather gaind on those who were pumping which made all hands impatient for the tryal. In the afternoon the ship was got under way with a gentle breeze of wind and stood in for the land; soon after the fother was finishd and applyd by fastning ropes to each Corner, then sinking the sail under the ship and with these ropes drawing it as far backwards as we could; in about ½ an hour to our great surprize the ship was pumpd dry and upon letting the pumps stand she was found to make very little water, so much beyond our most sanguine Expectations had this singular expedient succeeded. At night came to an anchor, the fother still keeping her almost clear so that we were in an instant raisd from almost despondency to the greatest hopes: we were now almost too sanguine talking of nothing but getting her into some harbour where we might lay her ashore and repair her, or if we could not find such a place we little doubted to the East indies.

During the whole time of this distress I must say for the credit of our people that I beleive every man exerted his utmost for the preservation of the ship, contrary to what I have universaly heard to be the behavior of sea men who have commonly as soon as a ship is in a desperate situation began to plunder and refuse all command. This was no doubt owing intirely to the cool and steady conduct of the officers, who during the whole

time never gave an order which did not shew them to be
perfectly composd and unmovd by the circumstances
howsoever dreadfull they might appear.

JUNE 13.   One Pump and that not half workd kept the ship
clear all night. In the morn we weighd with a fine breeze of
wind and steerd along ashore among innumerable shoals, the
boats keeping ahead and examining every appearance of a
harbour which presented itself; nothing however was met with
which could possibly suit our situation, bad as it was, so at
night we came to an anchor. The Pinnace however which had
gone far ahead was not returnd, nor did she till nine O'Clock,
when she reported that she had found just the place we
wanted, in which the tide rose sufficiently and there was every
natural convenience that could be wishd for either laying the
ship ashore or heaving her down. This was too much to be
beleivd by our most sanguine wishes: we however hopd that
the place might do for us if not so much as we had been told
yet something to better our situation, as yet but precarious,
having nothing but a lock of Wool between us and
destruction.

Cooktown

JUNE 14. Very fresh Sea breeze. A boat was sent ahead to shew
us the way into the harbour, but by some mistake of signals we
were obligd to come to an anchor again of the mouth of it
without going in, where it soon blew too fresh for us to
Weigh. We now began to consider our good fortune; had it
blown as fresh the day before yesterday or before that we could
never have got off but must inevitably have been dashd to
peices on the rocks. The Captn and myself went ashore to view
the Harbour and found it indeed beyond our most sanguine
wishes: it was the mouth of a river[48] the entrance of which was
to be sure narrow enough and shallow, but when once in the
ship might be moord afloat so near the shore that by a stage
from her to it all her Cargo might be got out and in again in
a very short time; in this same place she might be hove down
with all ease, but the beach gave signs of the tides rising in the
springs 6 or 7 feet which was more than enough to do our
business without that trouble. The meeting with so many
natural advantages in a harbour so near us at the very time of
our misfortune appeard almost providential; we had not in the

48. Endeavour River.

voyage before seen a place so well suited for our purpose as this was, and certainly had no right to expect the tides to rise so high here that did not rise half so much at the place where we struck, only 8 Leagues from this place; we therefore returnd on board in high spirits and raisd the spirits of our freinds on board as much as our own by bringing them the welcome news of aproaching security. It blew however too fresh to night for us to attempt to weigh the anchor, I even think as fresh as it has ever done since we have been upon the Coast.

JUNE 15. Blew all day as fresh as it did yesterday. We thought much of our good fortune in having fair weather upon the rocks when upon the Brink of such a gale. Our people were now however pretty well recoverd from their fatigues having had plenty of rest, as the ship since she was Fotherd has not made more water than one pump half workd will keep clear. At night we observd a fire ashore near where we were to lay, which made us hope that the necessary lengh of our stay would give us an oportunity of being acquainted with the Indians who made it.

JUNE 16. In the morn it was a little more moderate and we attempted to weigh but were soon obligd to vere away all that we had got, the wind freshning upon us so much. Fires were made upon the hills and we saw 4 Indians through our glasses who went away along shore, in going along which they made two more fires for what purpose we could not guess. Tupia whose bad gums were very soon followd by livid spots on his legs and every symptom of inveterate scurvy, notwithstanding acid, bark and every medecine our Surgeon could give him, became now extreemly ill; Mr Green[49] the astronomer was also in a very poor way, which made everybody in the Cabbin very desirous of getting ashore and impatient at our tedious delays.

49. Charles Green, died January 1771.

JUNE 17. Weather a little less rough than it was. Weighd and brought the ship in but in doing it ran her twice ashore by the narrowness of the channel; the second time she remaind till the tide lifted her off. In the meantime Dr Solander and myself began our Plant gathering. In the Evening the ship was moord

50. This was Cook Harbour, present-day Cooktown.

within 20 feet of the shore[50] afloat and before night much lumber was got out of her.

JUNE 18.   A stage was built from the ship which much facilitated our undertakings. Myself walking in the countrey saw old Frames of Indian houses and places where they had dressd shellfish in the same manner as the Islanders, but no signs that they had been at the place for 6 months at least. The countrey in general was sandy between the hills and barren made walking very easy; Musquetos there were some and but few, a peice of good fortune in a place where we were likely to remain some time. Tupia who had employd himself since we were here in angling and had livd intirely on what he caught was surprizingly recoverd. Poor Mr Green still very ill. Weather blowing hard with showers; had we not got in yesterday we certainly could not today.

JUNE 19.   Went over the Water today to spy the land which there was sand hills. On them I saw some Indian houses which seem'd to have been inhabited since those on this side, tho not very lately. There were vast flocks of Pigeons and crows; of the former which were very beautifull we shot several; the latter exactly like those in England were so shy that we could not come near them by any means. The Inlet or river in which we lay ran very far into the countrey, keeping its course over flat land overgrown with Mangroves; the countrey inland was however sufficiently hilly. Evening hard rain.

JUNE 20.   Weather cleard up so we began to gather and Dry plants of which we had hopes of as many as we could muster during our stay. Observd that in many parts of the inlet were large quantities of Pumice stones which lay a good way above the high water mark, Probably carried there by freshes or extrordinary high tides as they certainly came from the Sea. Before night the ship was lightned and we observd with great pleasure that the springs[51] which were now beginning to lift rose as high as we could wish.

51. Tides.

JUNE 21.   Fine clear weather: began today to lay Plants in sand. By night the ship was quite clear and in the nights tide (which we had constantly observd to be much higher than the days) we hauld her ashore.

JUNE 22.   In the morn I saw her leak which was very large: in the middle was a hole large enough to have sunk a ship with twice our pumps but here providence had most visibly workd in our favour, for it was in great measure pluggd up by a stone which was as big as a mans fist: round the Edges of this stone had all the water come in which had so near overcome us, and here we found the wool and oakum or fothering which had releivd us in so unexpected a manner. The effects of the Coral rock upon her bottom is dificult to describe but more to beleive; it had cut through her plank and deep into one of her timbers, smoothing the gashes still before it so that the whole might easily be imagind to be cut with an axe. Myself employd all day in laying in Plants. The People who were sent to the other side of the water in order to shoot Pigeons saw an animal as large as a grey hound, of a mouse coulour and very swift; they also saw many Indian houses and a brook of fresh water.

JUNE 23. The people who went over the River saw the animal again and describd him much in the same manner as yesterday.

JUNE 24.   Gathering plants and hearing descriptions of the animal which is now seen by every body. A seaman who had been out in the woods brought home the description of an animal he had seen composd in so Seamanlike a stile that I cannot help mentioning it: it was (says he) about as large and much like a one gallon cagg, as black as the Devil and had 2 horns on its head, it went but Slowly but I dard not touch it.[52]

52. This was perhaps a fruit bat or flying fox.

JUNE 25.   In gathering plants today I myself had the good fortune to see the beast so much talkd of, tho but imperfectly; he was not only like a grey hound in size and running but had a long tail, as long as any grey hounds; what to liken him to I could not tell, nothing certainly that I have seen at all resembles him.

JUNE 26. Since the ship has been hauld ashore the water that has come into her has of course all gone backwards and my plants which were for safety stowd in the bread room were this day found under water; nobody had warnd me of this danger which had never once enterd into my head; the mischeif was however now done so I set to work to remedy it to the best of my power. The day was scarce long enough to get them all shifted &c: many were savd but some intirely lost and spoild.

JUNE 27.   Some of the Gentlemen who had been out in the woods Yesterday brought home the leaves of a plant which I took to be *Arum Esculentum*, the same I beleive as is calld Coccos in the West Indies. In consequence of this I went to the place and found plenty; on tryal however the roots were found to be too acrid to be eat, the leaves however when boild were little inferior to spinage. In the same place grew plenty of Cabbage trees a kind of Wild Plantain whose fruit was so full of stones that it was scarce eatable, another fruit about as large as a small golden pippin but flatter, of a deep purple colour; these when gatherd off from the tree were very hard and disagreable but after being kept a few days became soft and tasted much like indiferent Damsons.

JUNE 28.   Tupia by Roasting his Coccos very much in his Oven made them lose intirely their acridity; the Roots were so small that we did not think them at all an object for the ship so resolvd to content ourselves with the greens which are calld in the West Indies Indian Kale. I went with the seamen to shew them the Place and they Gatherd a large quantity. Saw one tree and only one notchd in the same manner as those at Botany[53] bay. We have ever since we have been here observd the nests of a kind of Ants much like the White ants in the East indies but to us perfectly harmless; they were always pyramidical, from a few inches to 6 feet in hight and very much resembled stones which I have seen in English Druidical monuments. Today we met with a large number of them of all sizes rangd in a small open place which had a very pretty effect; Dr Solander compard them to the Rune Stones on the Plains of Upsal in Sweden, myself to all the smaller Druidical monuments I had seen.

53. Banks first wrote 'Stingrays' but has later revised his manuscript in the light of Cook's name change.

54. James Maria Magra. He later changed his name to Matra and produced a plan for colonising New South Wales. The Sydney suburb of Matraville is named after him.

JUNE 29. One of our Midshipmen[54] an American who was out a shooting today saw a Wolf, perfectly he sayd like those he had seen in America; he shot at it but did not kill it. The Seine was hauld today for the first time and 150 lb of Fish caught in it.

JUNE 30. The second lieutenant saw 2 animals like dogs but smaller, they ran like hares and were of a straw colour. Sein caught 213 lb of Fish.

July 1770

*... but the Musquetos, whose peacefull dominions it seems we had invaded,
sparð no pains to molest as much as was in their Power ...*

Endeavour River

55. Banks first wrote 'New
Jerusalem'. this was the
name given by Pedro
Fernandez de Quiros to the
city which he hoped to
found at Vanuatu when he
arrived there in 1606.
Quiros named the island
Espiritu Santo.

JULY 1. Being Sunday all hands were ashore on liberty, many animals were seen by them. The Indians had a fire about a league off up the river. O[u]r second Lieutenant found the husk of a Cocoa nut full of Barnacles cast up on the Beach; probably it had come from some Island to windward, From Terra del Espirito Santo[55] possibly as we are now in its latitude.

The ship was now finishd and tomorrow being the highest spring tide it was intended to haul her off, so we began to think how we should get out of this place, where so lately to get only in was our utmost ambition. We had observ'd in coming in innumerable shoals and sands all round us so we went upon a high hill to see what passage to the sea might be open. When we came there the Prospect was indeed melancholy: the sea every where full of innumerable shoals, some above and some under water, and no prospect of any streight passage out. To return as we came was impossible, the trade wind blew directly in our teeth; most dangerous then our navigation must be among unknown dangers. How soon might we again be reducd to the misfortune we had so lately escapd! Escapd indeed we had not till we were again in an open sea.

JULY 2. A great dew, which is the first we have had, and a Land breeze in the morn the first likewise. The Wild Plantain trees, tho their fruit does not serve for food, are to us a most material benefit; we made Baskets of their stalks (a thing we learnd of the Islanders) in which our plants which would not otherwise keep home remain fresh for 2 or 3 days; indeed in a hot climate it is hardly Practicable to go on without such baskets which we call by the Island name of *Papa Mya*. Our Plants dry better in Paper Books than in Sand, with this precaution, that one person is intirely employd in attending them who shifts them all once a day, exposes the Quires in which they are to the greatest heat of the sun and at night covers them most carefully up from any damps, always carefull not to bring them out too soon in a morning or leave them out too late in the evening. Tide rose not so high as was expected so the ship would not come off.

JULY 3. The Pinnace which had been sent out yesterday in search of a Passage returnd today, having found a way by which she past most of the shoals that we could see but not all. This Passage was also to windward of us so that we could only hope to get there by the assistance of a land breeze, of which we have had but one since we lay in the Place, so this discovery added little comfort to our situation. He had in his return landed on a dry reef where he found vast plenty of shell fish so that the Boat was compleatly loaded, cheifly with a large kind of Cockles (*Chama Gigas*)[56] One of which was more than 2 men could eat. Many indeed were larger; the Cockswain of the Boat a little man declard that he saw on the reef a dead shell of one so large that he got into it and it fairly held him. At night the ship floated and was hauld off; an Allegator was seen swimming along side of her for some time. As I was crossing the harbour in my small boat we saw many sholes of Gar fish leaping high out of the water, some of which leap'd into the boat and were taken.

JULY 4. The ship has been a good deal straind by laying so long as she has done with her head aground and her stern afloat; so much so that she has sprung a plank between decks abreast the main chains. At night however she was laid ashore again in order if possible to examine if she had got any damage near that place.

56. Giant clams.

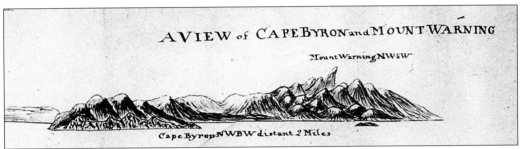

10. *Sketches of Mount Warning and Cape Byron.*

11. *Another of the plants collected from Botany Bay was this one,* Xylomelum pyriforme; *from the* Florilegium.

12. 'To compare it to any European animal would be impossible as it has not the least resemblance of any one I have seen.'

JULY 5. Went to the other side of the harbour and walkd along a sandy beach open to the trade wind. Here I found innumerable fruits, many of Plants I had not seen in this countrey; among them were some Cocoa nuts that had been open'd (as Tupia told us) by a kind of Crab, calld by the Dutch *Beurs Krabbe* (*Cancer Latro*) that feeds upon them. All these fruits were incrusted with sea productions and many of them Coverd with Barnacles, a sure sign that they have come far by sea, and as the trade wind blows almost right on shore they must have come from some other countrey — probably that discoverd by Quiros and calld Terra del Esprito Santo as the Latitudes according to his own account agree pretty well.

Tupia who parted from us and walkd away a shooting, on his return told us that he had seen 2 people who were digging in the ground for some kind of roots; on seeing him they ran away with great precipitation.

JULY 6. Set out today with the second lieutenant resolvd to Go a good way up the river and see if the countrey inland differd from that near the shore. We went for about 3 leagues among Mangroves, then we got into the countrey which differd very little from what we had seen. From hence we proceeded up the river which contracted itself much and lost most of its mangroves; the Banks were steep and coverd with trees of a Beautifull verdure particularly what is calld in the West Indies Mohoe or Bark tree (*Hibiscus tiliaceus*); the land within was generaly low, coverd thick with long grass, and seemd to promise great fertility were these people to plant and improve it. In the course of the Day Tupia saw a Wolf, so at least I guess by his description, and we saw 3 of the animals of the countrey but could not get one; also a kind of Batts as large as a Partridge but these also we were not lucky enough to get. At night we took up our lodgins close to the banks of the river and made a fire, but the Musquetos, whose peacefull dominions it seems we had invaded, spard no pains to molest as much as was in their Power: they followd us into the very smoak, nay almost into the fire, which hot as the Climate was we could better bear the heat of than their intolerable stings.

Between the hardness of our beds, the heat of the fire and the stings of these indefatigable insects the night was not spent so agreably but that day was earnestly wishd for by all of us; at last

JULY 7. it came and with its first dawn we set out in search of Game. We walkd many miles over the flats and saw 4 of the animals, 2 of which my greyhound fairly chas'd, but they beat him owing to the lengh and thickness of the grass which prevented him from running while they at every bound leapd over the tops of it. We observd much to our surprize that instead of Going upon all fours this animal went only upon two legs, making vast bounds just as the Jerbua (*Mus Jaculus*) does.[57] We returnd about noon and pursued our course up the river, which soon contracted itself into a fresh water brook where however the tide rose pretty considerably; towards evening it was so shallow being almost low water that we were obligd to get out of the boat and drag her, so finding a convenient place for sleeping in we resolvd to go no farther. Before our things were got up out of the boat we observd a smoak about a furlong from us: we did not doubt at all that the natives, who we had so long had a curiosity to see well, were there so three of us went immediately towards it hoping that the smallness of our numbers would induce them not to be afraid of us; when we came to the place however they were gone, probably upon having discoverd us before we saw them. The fire was in an old tree of touchwood; their houses were there, and branches of trees broken down with which the Children had been playing not yet wither'd; their footsteps also upon the sand below the high tide mark provd that they had very lately been there; near their oven, in which victuals had been dressd since morn, were shells of a kind of Clam and roots of a wild Yam which had been cookd in it. Thus were we disapointed of the only good chance we have had of seing the people since we came here by their unacountable timidity, and Night soon coming on we repair to our quarters, which was upon a broad sand bank under the shade of a Bush where we hopd the Musquetos would not trouble us. Our beds of plantain leaves spread on the sand as soft as a mattrass, our Cloaks for bedcloths and grass pillows, but above all the intire absence of Musquetos made me and I beleive all of us sleep almost without intermission; had the Indians came they would

57. The jerboa is an African rodent.

certainly have caught us all Napping but that was the least in our thoughts.

The land about this place was not so fertile as lower down, the hills rose almost immediately from the river and were barren, stony and sandey much like those near the ship. The river near us abounded much in fish who at sun set leapd about in the water much as trouts do in Europe but we had no kind of tackle to take them with.

JULY 8. At day light in the Morn the tide serving we set out for the ship. In our passage down met several flocks of Whistling Ducks of which we shot some; we saw also an Allegator of about 7 feet long come out of the Mangroves and crawl into the Water. By 4 O'Clock we arrivd at the ship where we heard that the Indians had been near them but not come to them; Yesterday they had made a fire about a mile and a half of and this morn 2 had appeard on the beach opposite to the ship. At night the Pinnace which had been sent in search of a Passage to leward returnd, she had been unsuccessfull in her main errand. Shoals innumerable she had met with, upon one of them was lucky enough to see a turtle which was pursued and many more were seen, so many that three were taken with only the Boat hook. The promise of such plenty of good provisions made our situation appear much less dreadfull; were we obligd to Wait here for another season of the year when the winds might alter we could do it without fear of wanting Provisions: this thought alone put every body in vast spirits.

JULY 9. Myself went turtling in hopes to have loaded our long boat, but by a most unacountable conduct of the officer not one turtle was taken. I however went ashore upon the reef, saw the large Cockles and gatherd many shells and sea productions. At night returnd with my small boat leaving the large one upon the reef who I was sure would catch no turtle.

JULY 10. Four Indians appeard on the opposite shore; they had with them a Canoe made of wood with an outrigger in which two of them embarkd and came towards the ship but stop'd at the distance of a long Musquet shot, talking much and very loud to us. We hollowd to them and waving made them all the signs we could to come nearer; by degrees they venturd almost insensibly nearer and nearer till they were quite along side, often holding up their Lances as if to shew us that if we usd them ill they had weapons and would return our attack. Cloth, Nails, Paper, &c &c. was given to them all which they took and put into the canoe without shewing the least signs of satisfaction: at last a small fish was by accident thrown to them on which they expressd the greatest joy imaginable, and instantly putting off from the ship made signs that they would bring over their comrades, which they very soon did and all four landed near us, each carrying in his hand 2 Lances and his stick to throw them with. Tupia went towards; they stood all in a row in the attitude of throwing their Lances; he made signs that they should lay them down and come forward without them; this they immediately did and sat down with him upon the ground. We then came up to them and made them presents of Beads, Cloth &c. which they took and soon became very easy, only Jealous if any one attempted to go between them and their arms. At dinner time we made signs to them to come with us and eat but they refusd; we left them and they going into their Canoe padled back to where they came from.

JULY 11. Indians came over again today, 2 that were with us yesterday and two new ones who our old acquaintance introduc'd to us by their names, one of which was Yaparico. Tho we did not yesterday Observe it they all had the Septum or inner part of the nose bord through with a very large hole, in which one of them had stuck the bone of a bird as thick as a mans finger and 5 or 6 inches long, an ornament no doubt tho to us it appeard rather an uncouth one. They brought with them a fish which they gave to us in return I suppose for the fish we had given them yesterday. Their stay was but short for some of our gentlemen being rather too curious in examining their canoe they went directly to it and pushing it off went away without saying a word. At night the boat which had been sent to the reef for turtle came home and brought 3.

JULY 12. Indians came again today and venturd down to Tupias Tent, where they were so well pleasd with their reception that three staid while the fourth went with the Canoe to fetch two new ones; they introduc'd their strangers (which they always made a point of doing) by name and had some fish given them. They receivd it with indifference, signd to our people to cook it for them, which was done, and they eat part and gave the rest to my Bitch. They staid the most part of the morning but never venturd to go above 20 yards from their canoe. The ribbands by which we had tied medals round their necks the first day we saw them were coverd with smoak; I suppose they lay much in the smoak to keep off the Musquetos. They are a very small people or at least this tribe consisted of very small people, in general about 5 feet 6 in hight and very slender; one we measurd 5 feet 2 and another 5 feet 9, but he was far taller than any of his fellows; I do not know by what deception we were to a man of opinion, when we saw them run on the sand about ¼ of a mile from us, that they were taller and larger than we were. Their colour was nearest to that of chocolate, not that their skins were so dark but the smoak and dirt with which they were all casd over, which I suppose servd them instead of Cloths, made them of that colour. Their hair was strait in some and curld in others; they always wore it croppd close round their heads; it was of the same consistence with our hair, by no means wooly or curld like that of Negroes. Their eyes were in many lively and their teeth even and good; of them they had compleat setts, by no means wanting two of their fore teeth as Dampiers New Hollanders did. They were all of them clean limn'd, active and nimble. Cloaths they had none, not the least rag, those parts which nature willingly conceals being exposd to view compleatly uncoverd; yet when they stood still they would often or almost allways with their hand or something they held in it hide them in some measure at least, seemingly doing that as if by instinct. They Painted themselves with white and red, the first in lines and barrs on different Parts of their bodies, the other in large patches. Their ornaments were few: necklaces prettyly enough made of shells, bracelets wore round the upper part of their arms, consisting of strings lapd round with other strings as what we Call gymp in England, a string no thicker than a packthread ticd round their bodies which was sometimes made of human hair, a peice of Bark tied over their forehead, and the preposterous bone in their noses which I have before mentiond were all that we observd. One had indeed one of his Ears bord, the hole being big enough to put a thumb through, but this was peculiar to that one man and him I never saw wear in it any ornament. Their language was totaly different from that of the Islanders; it sounded more like English in its degree of harshness tho it could not be calld harsh neither. They almost continualy made use of the word *Chircau*[58], which we conceivd to be a term of Admiration as they still usd it when ever they saw any thing new; also Cherr, tut tut tut tut tut, which probably have the same signification. Their Canoe was not above 10 feet long and very narrow built, with an outrigger fitted much like those at the Islands only far inferior; they in shallow waters set her on with poles, in deep paddled her with paddles about 4 feet long; she just carried 4 people so that the 6 who visited us today were obligd to make 2 embarkations. Their Lances were much like those we had seen in Botany[59] bay, only they were all of them single pointed, and some pointed with the stings of sting-rays and bearded with two or three beards of the same, which made them indeed a terrible weapon; the board or stick with which they flung them was also made in a neater manner.

After having staid with us the greatest part of the morning they went away as they came. While they staid 2 more and a young woman made their appearance upon the Beach; she was to the utmost that we could see with our glasses as naked as the men.

JULY 13. Two Indians came in their Canoe to the ship, staid by her a very short time and then went along shore striking fish. Our Boat returnd from the reef with one turtle and one large Sting ray.

JULY 14. Our second lieutenant who was a shooting today had the good fortune to kill the animal that had so long been the subject of our speculations.[60] To compare it to any European animal would be impossible as it has not the least resemblance of any one I have seen. Its fore legs are extreemly short and of no use to it in walking, its hind again as disproportionaly long; with these it hops 7 or 8 feet at each hop in the same manner as the Gerbua, to which animal indeed it bears much resemblance except in Size, this being in weight 38 lb and the Gerbua no larger than a common rat.

58. Beaglehole comments: 'A rendering, spelt in various ways by the journal-keepers, of the word *yir-ke*, an expression of surprise.'

59. Banks first wrote 'Stingrays' and later revised it.

60. Banks wrote in the margin 'Kill Kanguru'.

JULY 15. The Beast which was killd yesterday was today Dressd for our dinners and provd excellent meat. In the evening the Boat returnd from the reef bringing 4 Turtles, so we may now be said to swim in Plenty. Our Turtles are certainly far preferable to any I have eat in England, which must proceed from their being eat fresh from the sea before they have either wasted away their fat, or by unatural food which is given them in the tubs where they are kept given themselves a fat of not so delicious a flavour as it is in their wild state. Most of those we have caught have been green turtle from 2 to 300 lb weight: these when killd were always found to be full of Turtle Grass (a kind of Conferva I beleive); two only were Loggerheads which were but indifferent meat; in their stomachs were nothing but shells.

JULY 16. As the ship was now nearly ready for her departure Dr Solander and myself employd ourselves in winding up our Botanical Bottoms,[61] examining what we wanted, and making up our complement of specimens of as many species as possible. The Boat brought 3 Turtle again today, one of which was a male which was easily to be distinguishd from the female by the vast size of his tail, which was four times longer and thicker than hers; in every other respect they were exactly alike. One of our people on board the ship who has been a Turtler in the West Indies told me that they never sent male Turtle home to England from thence because they wasted in keeping much more than the females, which we found to be true.

61. To wind up one's bottom is to finish a job.

JULY 17. Tupia who was over the water by himself saw 3 Indians, who gave him a kind of longish roots about as thick as a mans finger and of a very good taste. On his return the Captn Dr Solander and myself went over in hopes to see them and renew our connections; we met with four in a canoe who soon after came ashore and came to us without any signs of fear. After receiving the beads &c that we had given them they went away; we attempted to follow them hoping that they would lead us to their fellows where we might have an opportunity of seeing their Women; they however by signs made us understand that they did not desire our company.

JULY 18. Indians were over with us today and seemd to have lost all fear of us and became quite familiar; one of them at our desire threw his Lance which was about 8 feet in Lengh — it flew with a degree of swiftness and steadyness that realy surprizd me, never being above 4 feet from the ground and stuck deep in at the distance of 50 paces. After this they venturd on board the ship and soon became our very good freinds, so the Captn and me left them to the care of those who staid on board and went to a high hill about Six miles from the ship; here we overlookd a great deal of sea to Leward, which afforded a melancholy prospect of the dificulties we were to encounter when we came out of our present harbour: in which ever direction we turnd our eyes shoals innumerable were to be seen and no such thing as any passage to sea but through the winding channels between them, dangerous to the last degree.

JULY 19. Ten Indians visited us today and brought with them a larger quantity of Lances than they had ever done before, these they laid up in a tree leaving a man and a boy to take care of them and came on board the ship. They soon let us know their errand which was by some means or other to get one of our Turtle of which we had 8 or 9 laying upon the decks. They first by signs askd for One and on being refusd shewd great marks of Resentment; one who had askd me on my refusal stamping with his foot pushd me from him with a countenance full of disdain and applyd to some one else; as however they met with no encouragement in this they laid hold of a turtle and hauld him forwards towards the side of the ship where their canoe lay. It however was soon taken from them and replacd. They nevertheless repeated the expiriment 2 or 3 times and after meeting with so many repulses all in an instant leapd into their Canoe and went ashore where I had got before them Just ready to set out plant gathering; they seizd their arms in an instant, and taking fire from under a pitch kettle which was boiling they began to set fire to the grass to windward of the few things we had left ashore with surprizing dexterity and quickness; the grass which was 4 or 5 feet high and as dry as stubble burnt with vast fury. A Tent of mine which had been put up for Tupia when he was sick was the only thing of any consequence in the way of it so I leapd

Parkinson del.   T. Chambers Sc.

Two of the Natives of New-Holland, Advancing to Combat.

13. *Banks was very interested in the indigenous peoples he encountered on his voyage:*
he recorded their diet, dress, weapons, manners and vocabulary with great accuracy. This 1773 engraving
was based on sketches done by Parkinson.

14. *The* Endeavour *was beached on the Endeavour River for one and a half months for repairs, after being dramatically holed on the Great Barrier Reef. The stay gave Banks ample time to collect specimens of plants and animals, and to observe the local Aborigines.*

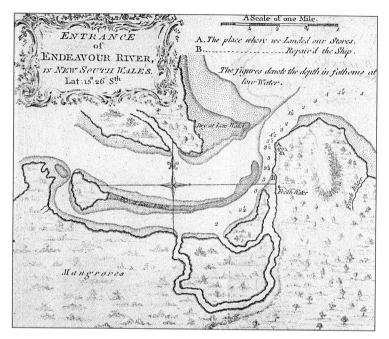

15. *Cook's charts of harbours and bays show not just his captain's eye for safe anchors, but his exceptional skill at surveying, sounding and mapping. This one of the Endeavour River is from Hawkesworth's official publication of the account of the* Endeavour *voyage.*

16. Dendrobium, *an orchid, from the* Florilegium.

into a boat to fetch some people from the ship in order to save it, and quickly returning hauld it down to the beach Just time enough. The Captn in the meantime followd the Indians to prevent their burning our Linnen and the Seine which lay on the grass just where they were gone. He had no musquet with him so soon returnd to fetch one for no threats or signs would make them desist. Mine was ashore and another loaded with shot, so we ran as fast as possible towards them and came just time enough to save the Seine by firing at an Indian who had already fird the grass in two places just to windward of it; on the shot striking him, tho he was full 40 yards from the Captn who fird, he dropd his fire and ran nimbly to his comrades who all ran off pretty fast. The Captn then loaded his musquet with a ball and fird it into the Mangroves abreast of where they ran to shew them that they were not yet out of our reach, they ran on quickning their pace on hearing the Ball and we soon lost sight of them; we then returnd to the Seine where the people who were ashore had got the fire under. We now thought we were free'd from these troublesome people but we soon heard their voices returning on which, anxious for some people who were washing that way, we ran towards them; on seeing us come with our musquets they again retird leasurely after an old man had venturd quite to us and said something which we could not understand. We followd for near a mile, then meeting with some rocks from whence we might observe their motions we sat down and they did so too about 100 yards from us. The little old man now came forward to us carrying in his hand a lance without a point. He halted several times and as he stood employd himself in collecting the moisture from under his arm pit with his finger which he every time drew through his mouth. We beckond to him to come: he then spoke to the others who all laid their lances against a tree and leaving them came forwards likewise and soon came quite to us. They had with them it seems 3 strangers who wanted to see the ship but the man who was shot at and the boy were gone, so our troop now consisted of 11. The Strangers were presented to us by name and we gave them such trinkets as we had about us; then we all proceeded towards the ship, they making signs as they came along that they would not set fire to the grass again and we distributing musquet balls among them and by our signs explaining their effect. When they came abreast of the ship they sat down but could not be prevaild upon to come on board, so after a little time we left them to their contemplations; they stayd about two hours and then departed.

We had great reason to thank our good Fortune that this accident happned so late in our stay, not a week before this our powder which was put ashore when first we came in had been taken on board, and that very morning only the store tent and that in which the sick had livd were got on board. I had little Idea of the fury with which the grass burnt in this hot climate, nor of the dificulty of extinguishing it when once lighted: this accident will however be a sufficient warning for us if ever we should again pitch tents in such a climate to burn Every thing round us before we begin.

JULY 20. Yesterday evening the ship was hauld off from the shore ready for her departure. In the night by some unlucky accident she taild ashore during the Ebb, and as the tide settled brought such a strain upon her rudder as alarmd us all greatly; the Tiller which was in the most danger beat hard under some strong sheep pens which had been built in a Platform over it; as the tide settled still more it came to the Point whether the tiller or Platform would Break, for one must, which the Platform fortunately did and made us at once easy. No Indians came near us but all the hills about us for many miles were on fire and at night made the most beautifull appearance imaginable. The Pinnace returnd which had been sent to Leeward in search of a Passage: the officer in her had met with nothing but shoals and not the least likelihood of a Passage that way, no very comfortable situation. Our ship it is true was now repaird: Leaky she was from the strains she had got but the water she made was trifling. We were ready to sail with the first fair wind but where to go? — to windward was impossible, to leward was a Labyrinth of Shoals, so that how soon we might have the ship to repair again or lose her quite no one could tell. Encounter the dificulty however we must and since our Bargain was a bad one make the Best of it. At night the Yawl returnd with one turtle in her: it had blown so much since she had been out that she with dificulty took even that, for as all our turtle had been taken by chasing moderate weather was absolutely necessary.

JULY 21. No signs of the Indians to day nor indeed any thing else worthy note.

JULY 22. The Turtle which was killd this morn had an Indian turtle peg in it which seemd to have laid there a long time. It was in the breast across the fore finns, having enterd at the soft part near the finns but the wound it had made in going in was intirely grown up; the peg itself was about 8 inches in lengh and as thick as a mans little finger. One of our people who had been sent out to gather Indian Kale straying from his party met with three indians, two men and a boy, he came upon them as they sat down among some long grass on a sudden and before he was aware of it. At first he was much afraid and offerd them his knife, the only thing he had which he thought might be acceptable to them; they took it and after handing it from one to another return'd it to him. They kept him about half an hour behaving most civily to him, only satisfying their curiosity in examining his body, which done they made him signs that he might go away which he did very well pleasd. They had hanging on a tree by them, he said, a quarter of the wild animal and a cocatoo; but how they had been clever enough to take these animals is almost beyond my conception, as both of them are most shy especialy the Cocatoos.

JULY 23. In Botanizing today on the other side of the river we accidentaly found the greatest part of the clothes which had been given to the Indians left all in a heap together, doubtless as lumber not worth carriage. May be had we lookd farther we should have found our other trinkets, for they seemd to set no value upon any thing we had except our turtle, which of all things we were the least able to spare them.

JULY 24. The blowing weather which had hinderd us from getting out several days still lasted, not at all to our satisfaction who had no one wish to remain longer in the place, which we had pretty well exhausted even of its natural history. The Dr and me were obligd to go very far for any thing new; to day we went several miles to a high hill where after sweating and broiling among the woods till night we were obligd to return almost empty. But the most vexatious accident imaginable befel us likewise: traveling in a deep vally, the sides of which were steep almost as a wall but coverd with trees and plenty of Brush wood, we found marking nuts (*anacardium orientale*) laying on the ground, and desirous as we were to find the tree on which they had grown, a thing that I beleive no European Botanist has seen, we were not with all our pains able to find it; so after cutting down 4 or 5 trees and spending much time were obligd to give over our hopes.

JULY 25. The Captn who was up the river today found the Canoe belonging to our freinds the Indians, which it seems they had left tied to some mangroves within a mile of the ship: themselves we could see by their fires were 5 or 6 miles off from us directly inland.

JULY 26. In botanizing to day I had the good fortune to take an animal of the Opossum (*Didelphis*) tribe: it was a female and with it I took two young ones. It was not unlike that remarkable one which De Bufon[62] has decribd by the name of Phalanger as an American animal; it was however not the same for De Buffon is certainly wrong in asserting that this tribe is peculiar to America; and in all probability, as Pallas has said in his *Zoologia*,[63] the Phalanger itself is a native of the East Indies, as my animal and that agree in the extrordinary conformation of their feet in which particular they differ from all the others.

62. Georges-Louis Leclerc de Buffon, *Histoire naturelle*, 1749–.

63. Peter Simon Pallas, *Miscellanea Zoologica*, 1766.

JULY 27. This day was dedicated to hunting the wild animal. We saw several and had the good fortune to kill a very large one which weighd 84 lb.

JULY 28. Botanizing with no kind of success. The Plants were now intirely compleated and nothing new to be found, so that sailing is all we wish for if the wind would but allow us. Dind today upon the animal, who eat but ill, he was I suppose too old. His fault however was an uncommon one, the total want of flavour, for he was certainly the most insipid meat I eat.

JULY 29. Went out again in search of the animals: our success today was not however quite so good as the last time, we saw few and killd one very small one which weighd no more than 8½ lb. My greyhound took him with ease tho the old ones where much too nimble for him.

JULY 30. Ever since the ship was hawld off for sailing we have had Blowing weather till today, when it changd to little wind and rain which gave us some hopes; in the evening however the wind returnd to its old Byas.

JULY 31. Morning cloudy and Boisterous enough; even clear with less wind which supplyd hopes at least for tomorrow.

August 1770

A Reef such a one as I now speak of is a thing scarcely known in Europe or indeed any where but in these seas: it is a wall of Coral rock rising almost perpendicularly out of the unfathomable ocean ...

Endeavour River

64. Warping is heaving or towing the ship, in this case into deep water.

AUGUST 1. During the Night it Blew as hard as ever; the Day was rainy with less wind but still not moderate enough for our undertakings.

AUGUST 2. Moderate and very rainy; great hopes that the Rain is a presage of approaching moderate weather.

AUGUST 3. In the morn our people were dubious about trying to get out and I beleive delayd it rather too long. At last however they began and warpd ahead[64] but desisted from their attempts after having ran the ship twice ashore.

AUGUST 4. Fine calm morn. Began early and warp'd the ship out, after which we saild right out till we came to the turtle reef where our turtlers took one turtle. Myself got some few shells but saw many Beautifull sea insects &c. At night our people who fishd caught abundance of sharks.

AUGUST 5. The Turtlers were again out upon the shoal and took one turtle. At 2 we weighd, resolvd to stand out as well as we could among the shoals, but before night were stoppd by another shoal which lay directly across our way.

AUGUST 6. Blew so fresh that we could not move but lay still all day, not without anxiety least the anchor should not hold.

AUGUST 7. During last night the gale had freshned much and in the morn we found that we had Drove above a League. Fortunately no shoal had in that distance taken us up but one was in sight astern and the ship drove fast towards it, on this another anchor was let go and much cable verd out but even this would not stop her. Our prospect was now more melancholy than ever: the shoal was plainly to be seen and the ship still driving gently down towards it, a sea running at the same time which would make it impossible ever to get off if we should be unfortunate enough to get on. Yards and Topmasts were therefore got down and every thing done which could be thought of to make the ship snug, without any effect: she still drove and the shoal we dreaded came nearer and nearer to us. The sheet anchor our last resource was now thought of and prepard, but fortunately for us before we were drove to the making use of that expedient the ship stoppd and held fast, to our great joy.[65] During the time of its blowing yesterday and today we became certain that between us and the open sea was a ledge of rocks or reef just the same as we had seen at the Islands, no very agreable discovery, for should that at any time join in with the main land we must wait for another season when different winds from the present ones prevaild; in which case we must infallibly be short of provisions or, if the turtle should fail us, Salt provisions without bread was all we had to trust to.

65. Detaching the yard-arms and the top masts was to reduce the wind resistance of the ship. A sheet anchor is usually a large canvas bag trailed in the water, its drag slowing movement.

AUGUST 8. The night Dark as pitch passd over not without much anxiety: whether our anchors held or not we could not tell and maybe might when we least thought of it be upon the very brink of destruction. Day light however releivd us shewd us that the anchors had held and also brought us rather more moderate weather, so that towards evening we venturd to get up Yards and top masts.

AUGUST 9. Night and morning still more moderate so that one anchor was got up and we had great hopes of sailing on the next morn.

AUGUST 10. Fine weather so the anchor was got up and we saild down to leward, convincd that we could not get out the way we had tried before and hoping there might be a passage

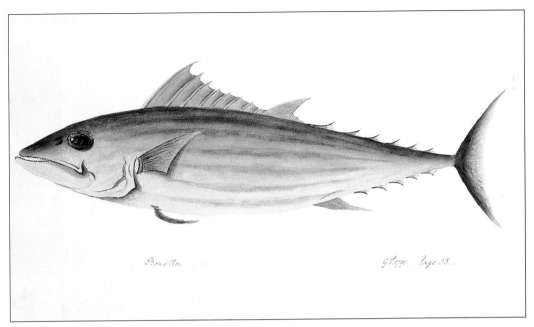

17. Bonetto

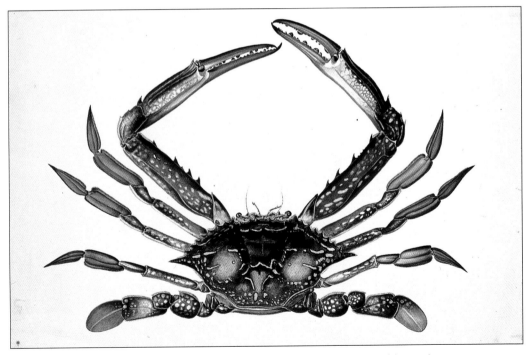

18. *Crabs were just some of the many different species collected by Banks*

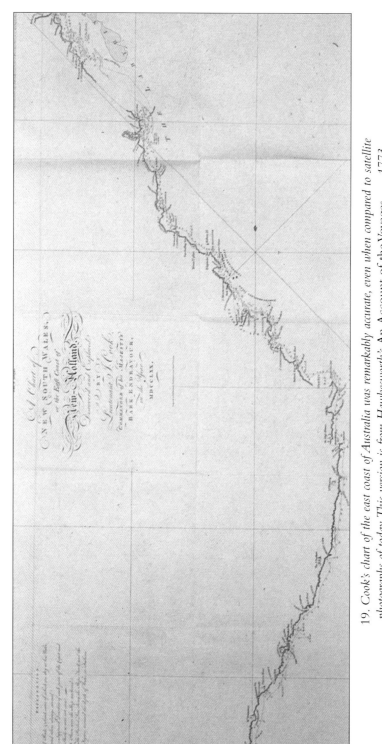

19. *Cook's chart of the east coast of Australia was remarkably accurate, even when compared to satellite photographs of today. This version is from Hawkesworth's An Account of the Voyages ... , 1773.*

66. South Direction, North Direction and Lizard Islands.

that way: in these hopes we were much encouraged by the sight of some high Islands[66] where we hopd the shoals would end. By 12 we were among these and fancied that the grand or outer reef ended on one of them so were all in high spirits, but about dinner time the people at the mast head saw as they thought Land all round us, on which we immediately came to an anchor resolvd to go ashore and from the hills examine whether it was so or not.

Cape Flattery

67. It was named Cape Flattery by Cook because they flattered themselves that they were free from danger, but they soon discovered otherwise.

The point we went upon was sandy and very Barren so it afforded very few plants or any thing else worth our observation.[67] The Sand itself indeed with which the whole countrey in a manner was coverd was infinitely fine and white, but till a glass house was built here that would turn to no account. We had the satisfaction however to see that what was taken for land round us provd only a number of Islands: to one very high one about 5 leagues from the Land the Captain resolvd to go in the Boat tomorrow in order to see whether the grand reef had realy left us or not.

Lizard Island

AUGUST 11. As propos'd yesterday the Captn went today to the Island which provd 5 leagues off from the ship, I went with him. In going out we passd over 2 very large shoals on which we saw great plenty of Turtle but we had too much wind to strike any. The Island itself was high; we ascended the hill and when we were at the top saw plainly the Grand Reef still extending itself Paralel with the shore at about the distance of 3 leagues from us or 8 from the main; through it were several channels exactly similar to those we had seen in the Islands. Through one of these we determind to [go] which seemd most easy: to ascertain however the Practicability of it We resolvd to stay upon the Island all night and at day break in the morn send the boat to sound one of them, which was accordingly done. We slept under the shade of a Bush that grew on the Beach very comfortably.

AUGUST 12. Great Part of yesterday and all this morn till the boat returnd I employd in searching the Island. On it I found some few plants which I had not before seen; the Island itself was small and Barren; on it was however one small tract of woodland which abounded very much with large Lizzards some of which I took. Distant as this Isle was from the main, the Indians had been here in their poor embarkations, sure sign that some part of the year must have very setled fine weather; we saw 7 or 8 frames of their huts and vast piles of shells the fish of which had I suppose been their food. All the houses were built upon the tops of Eminences exposd intirely to the SE, contrary to those of the main which are commonly placd under the shelter of some bushes or hill side to break off the wind. The officer who went in the Boat returnd with an account that the sea broke vastly high upon the reef and the swell was so great in the opening that he could not go into it to sound. This was sufficient to assure us of a safe passage out, so we got into the boat to return to the ship in high spirits, thinking our danger now at an end as we had a passage open for us to the main Sea. In our return we went ashore upon a low Island where we shot many birds; on it was an Eagles nest the young ones of which we killd, and another built on the ground by I know not what bird, of a most enormous magnitude — it was in circumference 26 feet and in hight 2 feet 8 built of sticks; the only Bird I have seen in this countrey capable of building such a nest seems to be the Pelecan.[68] The Indians have been here likewise and livd upon turtle, as we could plainly see by the heaps of Callipashes[69] which were pild up in several parts of the Island. Our Master who had been sent to leward to examine that Passage went ashore upon a low Island where he slept. Here he saw vast plenty of turtle shells, and so great plenty had the Indians had when there that they had hung up the finns with the meat left on them in trees, where the sun had dryd them so well that our seamen eat them heartily. He saw also two spots clear of grass which had lately been dug up; they were about 7 feet long and shapd like a grave, for which indeed he took them.

68. It was probably the nest of an osprey.

69. The upper shell of a turtle.

Cook's Passage

AUGUST 13. Ship stood out for the opening we had seen in the reef and about 2 O'Clock passd it. It was about ½ a mile wide. As soon as the ship was well without it we had no ground with 100 fathm of Line so became in an instant quite easy, being once more in the main Ocean and consequently freed from all our fears of shoals &c.

AUGUST 14. For the first time these three months we were this day out of sight of Land to our no small satisfaction: that very Ocean which had formerly been look'd upon with terror by (maybe) all of us was now the Assylum we had long wishd for and at last found. Satisfaction was clearly painted in every mans face: the day was fine and the trade wind brisk before which we steerd to the Northward; the well grown waves which followd the ship, sure sign of no land being in our neighbourhood, were contemplated with the greatest satisfaction, notwithstanding we plainly felt the effect of the blows they gave to our crazy ship, increasing her leaks considerably so that she made now 9 inches water every hour. This however was lookd upon as a light evil in comparison to those we had so lately made our escape from.

AUGUST 15. Fine weather and moderate trade. The Captn fearfull of going too far from the Land, least he should miss an opportunity of examining whether or not the passage which is layd down in some charts between New Holland and New Guinea realy existed or not,[70] steerd the ship west right in for the land; about 12 O'Clock it was seen from the Mast head and about one the Reef laying without it in just the same manner as when we left it. He stood on however resolving to stand off at night after having taken a nearer view, but just at night fall found himself in a manner embayd in the reef so that it was a moot Point whether or not he could weather it on either tack; we stood however to the Northward and at dark it was concluded that she would go clear of every thing we could see. The night however was not the most agreable: all the dangers we had escapd were little in comparison of being thrown upon this reef if that should be our lot. A Reef such a one as I now speak of is a thing scarcely known in Europe or indeed any where but in these seas: it is a wall of Coral rock rising almost perpendicularly out of the unfathomable ocean, always overflown at high water commonly 7 or 8 feet, and generaly bare at low water; the large waves of the vast ocean meeting with so sudden a resistance make here a most terrible surf Breaking mountain high, especialy when as in our case the general trade wind blows directly upon it.

70. Although Luis Vaez de Torres had sailed through the strait which now bears his name in 1606, he was unaware of the large land mass to the south. On board *Endeavour* was a copy of Charles de Brosses' work *Histoire des navigations aux terres australes* published in Paris in two volumes in 1756. This included charts by Robert de Vaugondy which depicted a strait. The map assumed an extended coastline east of the Dutch discoveries in the Gulf of Carpentaria and conjectured that there was a strait between this coast and New Guinea. Also on *Endeavour* was a copy of Alexander Dalrymple's *An account of the discoveries made in the South Pacifick Ocean, previous to 1764* published in 1769, an advance copy of which had been given to Banks in 1768, just prior to leaving. Torres' track south of New Guinea was shown on the chart which accompanied this work and Dalrymple claimed later to have given Banks information about Torres' voyage from a Spanish text.

AUGUST 16. At three O'Clock this morn it dropd calm on a sudden which did not at all better our situation: we judgd ourselves not more than 4 or 5 l'gs from the reef, maybe much less, and the swell of the sea which drove right in upon it carried the ship towards it fast. We tried the lead often in hopes to find ground that we might anchor but in vain; before 5 the roaring of the Surf was plainly heard and as day broke the vast foaming billows were plainly enough to be seen scarce a mile from us and towards which we found the ship carried by the waves surprizingly fast, so that by 6 o'Clock we were within a Cables lengh of them, driving on as fast as ever and still no ground with 100 fathm of line. Every method had been taken since we first saw our danger to get the boats out in hopes that they might tow us off but it was not yet acomplishd; the Pinnace had had a Plank strippd off her for repair and the longboat under the Booms was lashd and fastned so well from our suppos'd security that she was not yet got out. Two large Oars or sweeps were got out at the stern ports to pull the ships head round the other way in hopes that might delay till the boats were out. All this while we were approaching and came I beleive before this could be effected within 40 yards of the breaker; the same sea that washd the side of the ship rose in a breaker enormously high the very next time it did rise, so between us and it was only a dismal valley the breadth of one wave; even now the lead was hove 3 or 4 lines fastned together but no ground could be felt with above 150 fathm. Now was our case truly desperate, no man I beleive but who gave himself intirely over, a speedy death was all we had to hope for and that from the vastness of the Breakers which must quickly dash the ship all to peices was scarce to be doubted. Other hopes we had none: the boats were in the ship and must be dashd in peices with her and the nearest dry land was 8 or 10 Leagues distant. We did not however cease our endeavours to get out the long boat which was by this time almost accomplishd. At this critical juncture, at this I must say terrible moment, when all asistance seemd too little to save even our miserable lives, a small air of wind sprang up, so small that at any other time in a calm we should not have observd it. We however plainly saw that it instantly checkd our progress; every sail was therefore put in a proper direction to catch it and we just obse[r]vd the ship to move in a slaunting direction off from the breakers. This at least gave us time and redoubling our efforts we at last got out the long boat and manning her sent her a head. The ship still movd a little off but in less than 10 minutes our little Breeze died away into as flat a calm as ever. Now was our anziety again renewd: innumerable small peices of paper &c were thrown over the ships side to find whither the boats realy movd her ahead or not and so little did she move that it remain almost every other time a matter of dispute. Our little freindly Breeze now visited us again and lasted about as long as before, thrusting us possibly 100 yards farther from the breakers: we were still however in the very jaws of destruction. A small opening had been seen in the reef about a furlong from us, its breadth was scarce the lengh of the ship, into this however it was resolvd to push her if posible. Within was no surf, therefore we might save our lives: the doubt was only whether we could get the ship so far: our little breeze however a third time visited us and pushd us almost there. The fear of Death is Bitter: the prospect we now had before us of saving our lives tho at the expence of every thing we had made my heart set much lighter on its throne, and I suppose there were none but what felt the same sensations. At lengh we arrivd off the mouth of the wishd for opening and found to our surprize what had with the little breeze been the real cause of our Escape, a thing that we had not before dreamt of. The tide of flood it was that had hurried us so unacountably fast towards the reef, in the near neighbourhood of which we arrivd just at high water, consequently its ceasing to drive us any farther gave us the opportunity we had of getting off.[71] Now however the tide of Ebb made strong and gushd out of our little opening like a mill stream, so that it was impossible to get in; of this stream however we took the advantage as much as possible and it Carried us out near a quarter of a mile from the reef. We well knew that we were to take all the advantage possible of the Ebb so continued towing with all our might and with all our boats, the Pinnace being now repaird, till we had gott an offing of 1½ or 2 miles. By this time the tide began to turn and our suspence began again: as we had gaind so little while the ebb was in our favour we had some reason to imagine that the flood would hurry us back upon the reef in spite of our utmost endeavours. It was still as calm as ever so no likely hood of any wind today; indeed

71. Banks wrote here in the margin: 'saild into the opening'.

had wind sprung up we could only have searchd for another opening, for we were so embayd by the reef that with the general trade wind it was impossible to get out. Another opning was however seen ahead and the 1st Lieutenant[72] went away in the small boat to examine it. In the mean time we strugled hard with the flood, sometimes gaining a little then holding only our own and at others loosing a little, so that our situation was almost as bad as ever, as the flood had not yet come to its strengh. At 2 however the Lieutenant arrivd with news that the opening was very narrow: in it was good anchorage and a passage quite in free from shoals. The ships head was immediately put towards it and with the tide she towd fast so that by three we enterd and were hurried in by a stream almost like a mill race, which kept us from even a fear of the sides tho it was not above ¼ of mile in breadth.[73] By 4 we came to an anchor happy once more to encounter those shoals which but two days before we thought ourselves supreamly happy to have escap'd from. How little do men know what is for their real advantage: two days our utmost wishes were crownd by getting without the reef and today we were made again happy by getting within it.

AUGUST 17. As we were now safe at an anchor it was resolvd to send the boats upon the nearest shoal to search for shell fish, turtle or whatever else they could get. They accordingly went and Dr Solander and myself accompanied them in my small boat. In our way we met with two water snakes, one 5 the other 6 feet long; we took them both; they much resembled Land snakes only their tails were flatted sideways, I suppose for the convenience of swimming, and were not venomous. The shoal we went upon was the very reef we had so near been lost upon yesterday, now no longer terrible to us; it afforded little provision for the ship, no turtle, only 300lb of Great cockles, some were however of an immense size. We had in the way of curiosity much better success, meeting with many curious fish and mollusca besides Corals of many species, all alive, among which was the *Tubipora musica*. I have often lamented that we had not time to make proper observations upon this curious tribe of animals but we were so intirely taken up with the more conspicuous links of the chain of creation as fish, Plants, Birds &c &c. that it was impossible.

72. James Cook, here given his actual rank.

73. Called by Cook Providential Channel, for obvious reasons.

Temple Bay

74. Forbes's Isles were named after John Forbes, one of the commissioners of longitude.

AUGUST 18. Weighd and stood along shore with a gentle breeze, the main still 7 or 8 Leagues from us. In the even many shoals were ahead; we were however fortunate enough to find our way through them and at night anchord under an Island.[74] The tide here ran immensely strong which we lookd upon as a good omen: so strong a stream must in all probability have an outlet by which we could get out either on the South or North side of New Guinea. The smoothness of the water however plainly indicated that the reef continued between us and the Ocean.

Cape Grenville

75. Called by Cook Shelburne Bay. Sir William Petty, Earl of Shelburne, was Secretary of State for the Southern Department.

AUGUST 19. Weighd anchor and steerd as yesterday with a fresh trade wind. All morn were much entangled with Shoals, but so much do great dangers swallow up lesser ones that these once so much dreaded shoals were now look at with much less concern than formerly. At noon we passd along a large shoal on which the boats which were ahead saw many turtle but it blew to[o] fresh to catch them. We were now tolerably near the main, which appeard low and barren and often interspersd with large patches of the very white sand spoke of before.[75] On a small Island which we passd very near to were 5 natives, 2 of whoom carried their Lances in their hands; they came down upon a point and lookd at the ship for a little while and then retird.

Newcastle Bay

76. Luffing up means to sail close to the direction of the wind: bearing away is turning more with the wind.

AUGUST 20. Steering along shore as usual among many shoals, Luffing up for some and bearing away for others.[76] We are now pretty well experiencd in their appearances so as seldom to be deceivd and easily to know asunder a bottom colourd by white sand from a coral rock, the former of which, tho generaly in 12 or 14 fathom water, some time ago gave us much trouble. The reef was still supposd to be without us from the smoothness of our water. The mainland appeard very low and sandy and had many fires upon it, more than we had usualy observd. We passd during the day many low sandy Islands every one of which stood upon a large shoal; we have constantly found the best passage to lie near the main, and the farther from that you go near the reef the more numerous are the shoals. In the evening we observd the shoals to decrease in number but we still were in smooth water.

AUGUST 21. Running along shore with charming moderate weather, as indeed we have had ever since our second entering the reef. We observd both last night and this morn that the main lookd very narrow, so we began to look out for the Passage we expected to find between new Holland and New Guinea. At noon one was seen very narrow but appearing to widen: we resolv'd to try it so stood in. In passing through, for it was not more than a mile in lengh before it widned very much, we saw 10 Indians standing on a hill; 9 were armd with lances as we had been usd to see them, the tenth had a bow and arrows; 2 had also large ornaments of mother of Pearl shell hung round their necks.[77] After the ship had passd by 3 followd her, one of whoom was the bow man. We soon came abreast, from whence we concluded we might have a much better view than from our mast head, so the anchor was dropd and we prepard ourselves to go ashore to examine whether the place we stood into was a bay or a passage; for as we saild right before the trade wind we might find dificulty in getting out should it prove to be the former. The 3 Indians plac'd themselves upon the beach opposite to us as if resolvd either to oppose or assist our landing; when however we came about Musquet shot from them they all walkd leisurely away. The hill we were upon[78] was by much the most barren we had been upon; it however gave us the satisfaction of seeing a streight, at least as far as we could see, without any obstruction. In the Even a strong tide made us almost certain.

AUGUST 22. In the morn 3 or 4 women appeard upon the beach gathering shellfish: we lookd with our glasses and to us they appeard as they always did more naked than our mother Eve. The Ebb ran out so strong that we could not weigh till near noon. We had the Wind variable from N to W, the first time since we got the trade. Before we had proceeded far we met with a shoal which made us come to an anchor.[79]

AUGUST 23. In the morn calm: at nine however a small breeze sprang up on which we weighd and saild through a channel which had been found during the calm. At noon we were abreast of an Island which was white with the Dung of Birds; as we had little wind the ship was brought too we went ashore upon it and shot bobies till our ammunition was quite

77. Beaglehole comments: "From the description given it seems unlikely that these 'Indians' were Australian aborigines, who did not use the bow and arrow or have mother of pearl ornaments of this kind. They must have been Melanesians."

78. They were on Possession Island, where Cook claimed the eastern coast of New Holland for King George III, giving it the name New South Wales.

Endeavour Straits

79. Beaglehole identifies this as the Rothsay Banks.

Booby Island

expended. I myself Botanizd and found some plants which I had not before seen. After we came on board the winds were variable and soon after calm and very hot. Water still continued very Shoal but the swell, which ran larger than any we had met with within the reef, gave us great hopes.

AUGUST 24. Swell continued and in the morn the Best bower cable was broke in weighing by it. The whole day was spent in fruitless attempts to recover the anchor tho there was no more than 8 fathm water.

AUGUST 25. This morn by the first sweep the anchor was recoverd and we soon got under sail and lost sight of land with only 9 fathm water. At dinner met shoals which made us anchor again; in the eve however found a passage out and saild clear enough of them.

AUGUST 26. Fine weather and clear fresh trade. Stood to the W and deepned our water from 13 to 27. At night many Egg birds coming from the W.

Some account of that part of
New Holland now called
New South Wales

*H*aving now I beleive fairly Passd through between New Holland and New Guinea and having an open sea to the Westward, so that we tomorrow intend to steer more to the Northward in order to make the South Coast of New Guinea, it seems high time to take leave of New Holland, which I shall do by summing up together the few observations I have been able to make on the countrey and people. I much wishd indeed to have had better opportunities of seeing and observing the people, as they differ so much from the account that Dampier (the only man I know of who has seen them besides us) has given of them. He indeed saw them on a part of the coast very distant from where we were and consequently the people might be different; but I should rather conclude them to be the same, chiefly from having observd an universal conformity in such of their customs as came under my observation in the several places we landed upon during the run of 00[1] leagues along the coast. Dampier in general seems to be a faithfull relater, but in the voyage in which he touchd on the coast of New Holland he was in a ship of Pyrates, possibly himself not a little tainted by their idle examples: he might have kept no written Journal of any thing more than the navigation of the ship and when upon coming home he was sollicited to publish an account of his vogage have referrd to his memory for many particulars relating to people &c. These Indians when coverd with their filth which I beleive they never wash of are, if not coal black, very near it: as negroes then he might well esteem them and add the wooly hair and want of two fore teeth in consequence of the similitude in complexion between these and the natives of Africa; but from whatever cause it might arise, certain it is that

1. Banks probably did not know the precise figure, which was just under 670 leagues, or about 3200 kilometres.

Dampier either was mistaken very much in his account or else that he saw a very different race of people from those we have seen.

For the whole lengh of coast which we saild along there was a sameness to be observd in the face of the countrey very uncommon; Barren it may justly be calld and in a very high degree, that at least that we saw. The Soil in general is sandy and very light: on it grows grass tall enough but thin sett, and trees of a tolerable size, never however near together, in general 40, 50, or 60 feet assunder. This and spots sometimes very large of loose sand constitutes the general face of the countrey as you sail along it, and indeed of the greatest part even after you have penetrated inland as far as our situation would allow us to do. The Banks of the Bays indeed are generaly clothd with thick mangroves sometimes for a mile or more in breadth; the soil under these is rank mud always overflowd every spring tide. Inland you sometimes meet with a bog upon which the grass grows rank and thick so that no doubt the soil is sufficiently fertile. The Valleys also between the hills where runs of water come down are thick clothd with underwood, but they are generaly very steep and narrow, so that upon the Whole the fertile soil Bears no kind of Proportion to that which seems by nature doomd to everlasting Barrenness.

Water is here a scarce article or at least was so while we were there, which I beleive to have been in the very hight of the Dry season; some places we were in where we saw not a drop, and at the two places where we filld for the ships use it was done from pools not brooks. This drought is probably owing to the dryness of a soil almost intirely composd of sand in which high hills are scarce. That there is plenty however in the rainy season is sufficiently evincd by the channels we saw cut even in rocks down the sides of inconsiderable hills; these were in general dry, or if any of them contain water it was such as ran in the woody valleys, and these seldom carried water above half way down the hill. Some indeed we saw that formd brooks and ran quite down to the sea but these were scarce and in general brackish a good way up from the beach.

A Soil so barren and at the same time intirely void of the helps derivd from cultivation could not be supposd to yeild much towards the support of man. We had been so long at sea with but a scanty supply of fresh provisions that we had long usd to eat every thing we could lay our hands upon, fish, flesh, or vegetable which only was not poisonous; yet we could but now and then procure a dish of bad greens for our own table and never but in the place where the ship was careend met with a sufficient quantity to supply the ship. There indeed Palm cabbage and what is calld in the West Indies Indian Kale were in tolerable plenty, as was also a sort of Purslane. The other plants we eat were a kind of Beans, very bad, a kind of Parsley and a plant something resembling spinage, which two last grew only to the Southward. I shall give their botanical names as I beleive some of them were never eat by Europeans before: first Indian Kale (*Arum Esculentum*), Red flowerd purslane (*Sesuvium Portulacastrum*), Beans (*Glycine speciosa*), Parsley (*Apium*   ), Spinage (*Tetragonia cornuta*). Fruits we had still fewer; to the South was one something resembling a heart cherry only the stone was soft (*Eugenia*   )[2] which had nothing but a light acid to recommend it; to the Northward again a kind of Figs growing from the stalk of a tree, very indifferent (*Ficus caudiciflora*), a fruit we calld Plumbs like them in Colour but flat like a little cheese (   ), and another much like a damson both in appearance and taste; both these last however were so full of a large stone that eating them was but an unprofitable business. Wild Plantanes we had also but so full of seeds that they had little or no pulp.

For the article of timber, there is certainly no want of trees of more than the midling size and some in the valleys very large, but all of a very hard nature; our carpenters who cut them down for fire wood complaind much that their tools were damagd by them. Some trees there were also to the Northward whose soft bark, which easily peels off, is in the East Indies applyd to the use of calking ships in Lieu of Oakum.[3]

Palms here were of three different sorts. The first which grew plentifully to the Southward had leaves pleated like a fan; the Cabbage of these was small but exquisitely sweet and the nuts which it bore in great abundance a very good food for hogs.

2. Beaglehole suggests that this was *Eugenia banksii:*. 'Though no mention of Banks's brief note was made at the publication of this species 132 years after its collection, this is very likely the fruit in question.'

3. Possibly Queensland tea-tree.

The second was very much like the real cabbage tree of the West Indies, bearing large pinnated leaves like those of a Cocoa nut; these too yeilded cabbage if not so sweet as the other sort yet the quantity made ample amends. The third which as well as the second was found only in the Northern parts was low, seldom ten feet in hight, with small pennated leaves resembling those of some kinds of fern; Cabbage it had none but generaly bore a plentifull Crop of nutts about the size of a large chestnut and rounder. By the hulls of these which we found plentifully near the Indian fires we were assurd that these people eat them, and some of our gentlemen tried to do the same, but were deterrd from a second experiment by a hearty fit of vomiting and purging which was the consequence of the first. The hogs however who were still shorter of provision than we were eat them heartily and we concluded their constitutions stronger than ours, till after about a week they were all taken extreemly ill of indigestions; two died and the rest were savd with dificulty.

Other usefull plants we saw none, except perhaps two might be found so which yeild resin in abundance: the one a tree tolerably large with narrow leaves not unlike a willow which was very plentyfull in every place into which we went; this yeilded a blood red resin or rather gum-resin very nearly resembling *Sanguis draconis*, indeed as *Sanguis draconis* is the produce of several different plants this may perhaps be one of the sorts. This I should suppose to be the gum mentiond by Dampier[4] in his voyage round the world p.   and by him compard with *sanguis draconis*, as possibly also that which Tasman saw upon Diemens Land, where he says he saw gum of the trees and gum Lac of the ground; See his voyage in a collection publishd at London in 1694 p.133.[5] The other was a small plant with long narrow grassy leaves and a spike of flowers resembling much that kind of Bulrush which is cald in England Cats tail; this yeilded a resin of a bright yellow colour perfectly resembling Gambouge only that it did not stain; it had a sweet smell but what its properties are the chymists may be able to determine.[6]

Of Plants in general the countrey afforded a far larger variety than its barren appearance seemd to promise. Many of these

4. William Dampier, *A New Voyage Round the World*, 1697.

5. This was a published, abbreviated English version of Abel Tasman's voyage of 1642–43 on which he discovered Tasmania and the west coast of New Zealand.

6. The plant is a Grasstree: gamboge is a yellow tree resin from Indochina.

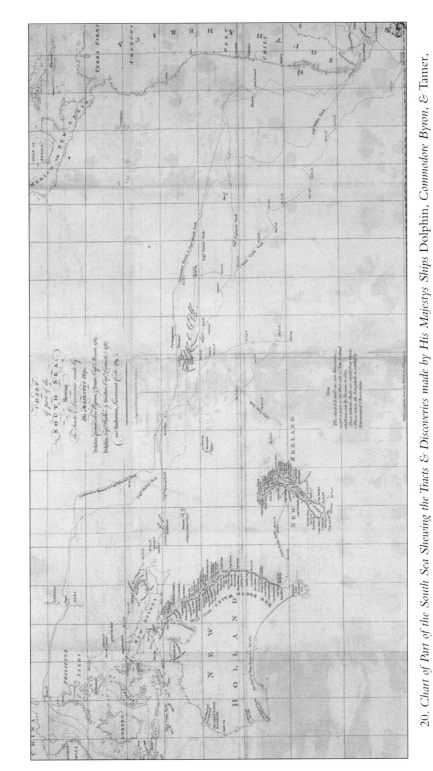

20. *Chart of Part of the South Sea Shewing the Tracts & Discoveries made by His Majestys Ships Dolphin, Commodore Byron, & Tamer, Capt Mouat, 1765, Dolphin, capn Wallis, & Swallow, Capn Carteret, 1767, and Endeavour, Lieutenant Cook, 1769; from Hawkesworth's An Account of the Voyages … , 1773.*

21. *Sir Joseph Banks in about 1809: a more formal portrait to the earlier one from 1774.*

have no doubt properties which might be usefull, but for Physical and œconomical purposes which we were not able to investigate, could we have understood the Indians or made them by any means our freinds we might perchance have learnt some of these; for tho their manner of life, but one degree removd from Brutes, does not seem to promise much yet they had a knowledge of plants as we plainly could percieve by their having names for them.

Thus much for plants: I have been rather particular in mentioning those which we eat hoping that such a remembrance might be of use to some or other into whose hands these papers may fall. For quadrupedes, Birds, fish &c. I shall say no more than that we had some time ago learnd to eat every identical species which came in our way: a hawk or a crow was to us as delicate and perhaps a better relishd meal than a partridge or Pheasant to those who have plenty of dainties: we wanted nothing to reccomend any food but its not being salt, that alone was sufficient to make it a delicacy. Shaggs, Sea gulls and all that tribe of sea fowl which are reccond bad from their trainy[7] or fishy taste were to us an agreable food, we did not at all taste the rankness, which no doubt has been and possibly will again be highly nauseous to us whenever we have plenty of Beef and mutton &c.

Quadrupeds we saw but few and were able to catch few of them that we did see. The largest was calld by the natives *Kangooroo*. It is different from any European and indeed any animal I have heard or read of except the Gerbua of Egypt, which is not larger than a rat when this is as large as a midling Lamb; the largest we shot weighd 84 lb. It may however be easily known from all other animals by the singular property of running or rather hopping upon only its hinder legs carrying its fore bent close to its breast; in this manner however it hops so fast that in the rocky bad ground where it is commonly found it easily beat my grey hound, who tho he was fairly started at several killd only one and that quite a young one. Another was calld by the natives *Je-Quoll*: it is about the size and something like a polecat, of a light brown spotted with white on the back and white under the belly.[8] The third was of the Opossum kind and much resembling that

7. This means like train oil, which was produced by boiling down blubber.

8. A native cat, the Aboriginal name of which is *dekol*.

calld by De Buffon Phalanger. Of these two last I took only one individual of each. Batts here were many. One small we took which was much like if not identicaly the same as that describd by de Buffon under the name of *Fer de cheval*; Another sort was as large or larger than a partrige but of this Species we were not fortunate enough to take one; we supposd it however to be either the *Roupette* or *Rougette* of the same author. Besides these Wolves[9] were I beleive seen by several of our people and some other animals describd, but from the unintelligible stile of the describers I could not even determine whether they were such as I myself had seen or of different kinds. Of these describtions I shall insert one as it is not unentertaining. A Seaman who had been out on duty on his return declard that he had seen an animal about the size of and much like a one gallon cagg; it was, says he, as black as the Devil and had wings, indeed I took it for the Devil or I might easily have catchd it for it crauld very slowly through the grass. After taking some pains I found out that the animal he had seen was no other than the Large Bat.

Birds there were Several Species of — sea fowl, Gulls, Shaggs, Soland geese or Gannets of 2 sorts, Bobies, &c. and Pelicans of an enormous size, but these last tho we saw many thousands of them were so shy that we never got one of them; as were the Cranes also of which we saw several very Large and some beautifull species. In the Rivers were ducks who flew in large flocks but were very hard to come at, and on the Beach were curlews of several sorts, some very like our English ones, and Many small Beach Birds. The Land Birds were crows, very like if not quite the same as our English ones, Parrots and Paraquets most Beautifull, White and black Cocatoes, Pidgeons, beautifull Doves, Bustards, and many others which did not at all resemble those of Europe. Most of these were extremely shy so that it was with dificulty that we shot any of them; a Crow in England tho in general sufficiently wary is I must say a fool to a New Holland crow and the same may be said of almost if not all the Birds in the countrey. The only ones we ever got in any plenty was Pidgeons of which we met Large flocks, of which the men who were sent out on purpose would sometimes kill 10 or 12 a day; they were a Beautifull Bird crested differently from any other Pidgeon I have seen. What

9. The partridge-sized bats were perhaps flying foxes; the wolves were no doubt dingoes.

can be the reason of this extrordinary shyness in the Birds is dificult to say, unless perhaps the Indians are very clever in deceiving them which we have very little reason to suppose, as we never saw any instrument with them but their Lances with which a Bird could be killd or taken, and these must be very improper tools for the Purpose; yet one of our people saw a white Cocatoe in their Possession which very bird we lookd upon to be one of the waryest of them all.

Of insects here were but few sorts and among them only the Ants were troublesome to us. Musquetos indeed were in some places tolerably plentyfull but it was our good fortune never to stay any time in such places, and where we did to meet with very few. The ants however made ample amends for the want of them, 2 sorts in particular: one green as a leaf and living upon trees where he built his nest, in size between that of a mans head and his fist, by bending the leaves together and glueing them with a whiteish papery substance which held them firmly together. In doing this their mangement was most curious: they bend down leaves broader than a mans hand and place them in such a direction as they chose, in doing of which a much larger force is necessary than these animals seem capable of. Many thousands indeed are employd in the joint work; I have seen them holding down such a leaf, as many as could stand by one another each drawing down with all his might while others within were employd to fasten the glue. How they had bent it down I had not an opportunity of seeing, but that it was held down by main strengh I easily provd by disturbing a part of them, on which the leaf bursting from the rest returnd to its natural situation and I had an opportunity to try with my finger the strengh that these little animals must have usd to get it down. But industrious as they are their courage if possible excells their industry; if we accidentaly shook the branches on which such nest were hung thousands would immediately throw themselves down, many of which falling upon us made us sensible of their stings and revengefull dispositions, especialy if as was often the case they got posession of our necks and hair. Their stings were by some esteemd not much less painfull than those of a bee, the pain however lasted only a few seconds. Another sort there were quite black whose manner of living was most extrordinary.

10. Banks leaves a space
here, no doubt intending to
enter a more exact
description of the tree later.

11. George Everhard
Rumph, *Herbarium
Amboinense*, Amsterdam,
1741.

12. Banks left a space in the
manuscript no doubt
intending to insert a more
exact description later.

They inhabited the inside of the Branches of one sort of tree, [10] the pith of which they hollowd out almost quite to the ends of the Branches; nevertheless the tree flourishd as well to all appearance as if no such accident had happned to it. When first we found the tree we of course gatherd the branches and were surprizd to find our hands instantly coverd with legions of these small animals who stung most intolerably; experience however taught us to be more carefull for the future. Rumphius mentions a similar instance to this in his *Herbarium Amboinense* Vol. II. p. 257[11]; his tree however does not at all resemble ours. A third sort nested in the inside of the root of a Plant [12] which grew on the Bark of trees in the same manner as Miseltoe; the root was as large as a large turnip and often much larger; when cut the inside shewd innumerable winding passages in which these animals livd; the plant itself throve to all appearance not a bit the worse for its numerous inhabitants. Several hundreds have I seen and never one but what was inhabited, tho some were so young as not to be much larger than a hasel nut. The ants themselves were very small, not above half as large as our red ants in England. They stung indeed but so little that it was scarce to be felt: the cheif inconvenience in handling the roots came from the infinite number, myriads would come in an instant out of many holes and running over the hand tickle so as to be scarce endurable. Rumphius has an account of this very bulb and its ants in the 6th Vol. p. 120, where he describes also another sort the ants of which are black. The fourth sort were perfectly harmless, at least they provd so to us tho they resembled almost minutely the white ants of the East Indies, the most mischevous Insect I beleive known in the world. Their architecture was however far superior to that of any other species. They had two kinds of Houses, one suspended on the Branches of trees, the other standing upright on the ground. The first sort were generaly 3 or 4 times as large as a mans head; they were built of a brittle substance seemingly made of small parts of vegetables kneaded together with some glutinous matter, probably afforded by themselves; on breaking this outer crust innumerable cells appeard full of inhabitants in winding directions, communicating with each other as well as with divers doors which led from the nest. From each of these went a passage archd over leading to different parts of the tree and generaly one large one to the ground; this I am inclind to beleive communicated with the other kind of house, for as the animals inhabiting both were precisely the same I see no reason why they should be supposd, contrary to Every instance that I know in nature, to build two different kinds of houses unless according to the conveniences of season, prey &c, they inhabited both equaly. This other kind of house which I now speak of was very often built near the foot of a tree, the Bark of which tree always had upon it their coverd ways tho but seldom the first kind of house; it was formd like an irregularly sided Cone and sometimes was more than 6 feet high and near as much in diameter; the smaller ones were generaly flat sided and resembled very much the old stones which are seen in many parts of England and supposd to be remains of Druidical worship. The outside Coat of these was 2 inches thick at least, of hard well temperd clay, under which were their cells; to these no doors were to be seen. All their passages were underground, where probably they were carried on till the root of some tree presented itself, up which they ascended and so up the trunk and branches by the coverd way before mentiond. These I should suppose to be the houses to which they retire in the winter season as they are undoubtedly able to defend them from any rain that can fall, while the others, tho generaly built under the shelter of some overhanging branch, must be but ill proof to a heavy rain from the thinness of their covering. Thus much for the ants, an industrious race who in all countries have for that reason been admird by man, tho probably in no countrey more admirable than in this. The few observations have wrote down of them are cheifly from conjecture and therefore are not at all to be depended upon; was any man however to be setled here who had time and inclination to observe their œconomy I am convincd it would far exceed that of any insects we know, not excepting our much admird bees.

The sea however made some amends for the Barreness of the Land. Fish tho not so plentyfull as they generaly are in higher latitudes were far from scarce; where we had an opportunity of haling the Seine we generaly caught from 50 to 200 lb of fish in a tide. There sorts were various, none I think but Mullets known in Europe; in general however they were sufficiently

palatable and some very delicate food; the Sting rays indeed
which were caught on the Southern part of the coast were
very coarse, but there little else was caught so we were obligd
to comfort ourselves with the comforts of Plenty and enjoy
more pleasure in Satiety than in eating. To the Northward
again when we came to be entangled within the great Reef
(within which we saild to our knowledge 0^{13} Leages and we
knew not how many more, perplexd every moment with
shoals) was a plenty of Turtle hardly to be credited, every
shoal swarmd with them. The weather indeed was generaly so
boisterous that our boats could not row after them so fast as
they could swim, so that we got but few, but they were
excellent and so large that a single Turtle always servd the ship.
Had we been there either at the time of Laying or the more
moderate season we doubtless might have taken any quantity.
Besides this all the shoals that were dry at half Ebb afforded
plenty of fish that were left dry in small hollows of the rocks,
and a profusion of Large shell fish (*Chama Gigas*) such as
Dampier describes Vol III, p. 191.[14] The large ones of this kind
had 10 or 15 lb of meat in them; it was indeed rather strong
but I beleive a very wholesome food and well relishd by the
people in general. On different parts of the Coast were also
found oysters which were said to be very well tasted; the shells
also of well sizd Lobsters and crabs were seen but these it was
never our fortune to catch.

Upon the whole New Holland, tho in every respect the most
barren countrey I have seen, is not so bad but that between the
productions of sea and Land a company of People who should
have the misfortune of being shipwreckd upon it might
support themselves, even by the resources that we have seen.
Undoubtedly a longer stay and visiting different parts would
discover many more.

This immense tract of Land, the largest known which does not
bear the name of a continent, as it is considerably larger than
all Europe, is thinly inhabited even to admiration, at least that
part of it that we saw: we never but once saw so many as thirty
Indians together and that was a family, Men women and
children, assembled upon a rock to see the ship pass by. At
Sting-Rays bay where they evidently came down to fight us

several times they never could muster above 14 or 15 fighting men, indeed in other places they generaly ran away from us, from whence it might be concluded that there were greater numbers than we saw, but their houses and sheds in the woods which we never faild to find convincd us of the smallness of their parties. We saw indeed only the sea coast: what the immense tract of inland countrey may produce is to us totaly unknown: we may have liberty to conjecture however that they are totaly uninhabited. The Sea has I beleive been universaly found to be the cheif source of supplys to Indians ignorant of the arts of cultivation: the wild produce of the Land alone seems scarce able to support them at all seasons, at least I do not remember to have read of any inland nation who did not cultivate the ground more or less, even the North Americans who were so well versd in hunting sowd their Maize. But should a people live inland who supported themselves by cultivation these inhabitants of the sea coast must certainly have learn'd to imitate them in some degree at least, otherwise their reason must be supposd to hold a rank little superior to that of monkies.

Whatever may be the reason of this want of People is dificult to guess, unless perhaps the Barreness of the Soil and scarcity of fresh water; but why mankind should not increase here as fast as in other places unless their small tribes have frequent wars in which many are destroyd; they were indeed generaly furnishd with plenty of weapons whose points of the stings of Sting-Rays seemd intended against nothing but their own species, from whence such an inference might easily be drawn.

That their customs were nearly the same throughout the whole lengh of the coast along which we saild I should think very probable. Tho we had Connections with them only at one place yet we saw them either with our eyes or glasses many times, and at Sting Rays bay had some experience of their manners; their Colour, arms, method of using them, were the same as we afterwards had a nearer view of; they likewise in the same manner went naked, and painted themselves, their houses were the same, they notchd large trees in the same manner and even the bags they carried their furniture in were of exactly the same manufacture, something between netting and Knitting which I have no where else seen in the intermediate places. Our glasses might deceive us in many things but their colour and want of cloths we certainly did see and wherever we came ashore the houses and sheds, places where they had dressd victuals with heated stones, and trees notchd for the convenience of climbing them sufficiently evincd them to be the same people.

The tribe with which we had connections consisted of 21 people, 12 men 7 women a boy and a girl, so many at least we saw and there might be more, especialy women, who we did not see. The men were remarkably short and slender built in proportion; the tallest we measurd was 5 feet 9, the shortest 5–2; their medium hight seemd to be about five feet six, as the tall man appeard more disproportioned in size from his fellows than the short one. What their absolute colour is is difficult to say, they were so compleatly coverd with dirt, which seemd to have stuck to their hides from the day of their birth without their once having attemptd to remove it; I tryd indeed by spitting upon my finger and rubbing but alterd the colour very little, which as nearly as might be resembled that of Chocolate. The beards of several were bushy and thick; their hair which as well as their beards was black they wore croppd close round their ears; in some it was lank as a Europeans, in others a little crispd as is common in the South sea Islands but in none of them at all resembling the wool of Negroes. They had also all their fore teeth; in which two things they differ cheifly from those seen by Dampier; supposing him not to be mistaken. As for colour they would undoubtedly be calld blacks by any one not usd to consider attentively the colours of different Nations; myself should never have thought of such distinctions had I not seen the effect of Sun and wind upon the natives of the South sea Islands, where many of the Better sort of people who keep themselves close at home are nearly as white as Europeans, while the poorer sort, obligd in their business of fishing &c. to expose their naked bodies to all the inclemencies of the Climate, have some among them but little lighter than the New Hollanders.[15] They were all to a man lean and clean limnd and seemd to be very light and active; their countenances were not without some expression tho I cannot charge them with much, their voices in general shrill and effeminate.

15. Banks has added a marginal note to the manuscript: 'Bourgainvile 2 species'. Beaglehole comments: 'a reference to Bougainville's observation that there seemed to be two races in Tahiti, one tall and impressive...; and the other shorter and as dark as mulattos – though they had the same language, the same customs, and mixed without distinction'. Louis Antoine de Bougainville's expedition was in the Pacific a few years earlier in 1768, at one time only about 400 kilometres east of Cooktown, but failed to find the east coast of Australia. His published account appeared in 1771, so this marginal note is a later thought by Banks.

Of Cloths they had not the least part but naked as ever our general father was before his fall, they seemd no more conscious of their nakedness than if they had not been the children of Parents who eat the fruit of the tree of knowledge. Whether this want of what most nations look upon as absolutely necessary proceeds from idleness or want of invention is difficult to say; in the article of ornaments however, useless as they are, neither has the one hinderd them from contriving nor the other from making them. Of these the cheif and that on which they seem to set the greatest value is a bone about 5 or 6 inches in lengh and as thick as a mans finger, which they thrust into a hole bord through that part which divides the nostrils so that it sticks across their face, making in the eyes of Europeans a most ludicrous appearance, tho no doubt they esteem even this as an addition to their beauty which they purchasd with hourly inconvenience; for when this bone was in its place, or as our seamen termd it their spritsail yard was riggd across, it compleatly stop'd up both nostrils so that they spoke in the nose in a manner one should think scarce intelligible. Besides these extrordinary bones they had necklaces made of shells neatly enough cut and strung together, bracelets also if one may call by that name 4 or 5 ring of small cord wore round the upper part of the arm, also a belt or string tied round the waist about as thick as worsted yarn, which last was frequently made of either human hair or that of the Beast calld by them Kangooroo. Besides these they paint themselves with the colours of red and white: the red they commonly lay on in broad patches on their shoulders or breasts; the white in stripes some of which were narrow and confind to small parts of their body, others were broad and carried with some degree of taste across their bodies, round their legs and arms &c; they also lay it on in circles round their eyes and in patches in different parts of their faces. The red they usd seemd to be red ocre but what the white was we could not find out; it was heavy and close graind almost as white lead and had a saponaceos feel, possibly it might be a kind of Steatites.[16] We lamented not being able to procure a bit to examine. These people seemd to have no Idea of traffick nor could we teach them; indeed it seemd that we had no one thing on which they set a value equal to induce them to part with the smallest trifle; except one fish which weighd about

16. 'saponaceous' is soapy; the white powder was kaolin, a type of clay.

½ a pound that they brought as a kind of token of peace no one in the ship I beleive procurd from them the smallest article. They readily receivd the things we gave them but never would understand our signs when we askd for returns. This however must not be forgot, that whatever opportunities they had they never once attempted to take any thing in a clandestine manner; whatever they wanted they openly askd for and in almost all cases bore the refusal if they met with one with much indifference, except Turtles.

Dirty as these people are they seem to be intirely free from Lice, a circumstance rarely observd among the most cleanly Indians, and which here is the more remarkable as their hair was generaly Matted and filthy enough. In all of them indeed it was very thin and seemd as if seldom disturbd with the Combing even of their fingers, much less to have any oil or grease put into it; nor did the custom of oiling their bodies, so common among most uncivilizd nations, seem to have the least footing here.

On their bodies we observd very few marks of cutaneous disorders as scurf, scars of sores &c. Their spare thin bodies indicate a temperance in eating, the consequence either of necessity or inclination, equaly productive of health particularly in this respect. On the fleshy parts of their arms and thighs and some of their sides were large scars in regular lines, which by their breadth and the convexity with which they had heald shewd plainly that they had been made by deep cuts of some blunt instrument, a shell perhaps or the edge of a broken stone. These as far as we could understand by the Signs they made use of were the marks of their Lamentations for the deceasd, in honour to whose memory or to shew the excess of their greif they had in this manner wept for in blood.[17]

17. The scars are more likely to have been initiation marks.

For Food they seem to depend very much tho not intirely upon the Sea. Fish of all kinds, Turtle and even crabs they strike with their Lances very dextrously. These are generaly bearded with broad beards and their points smeard over with a kind of hard resin which makes them peirce a hard body far easier than they would do without it. In the sourthern parts these fish spears had 4 prongs and besides the resin were pointed with the sharp bone of a fish; to the Northward again their spears had only one point; yet both I beleive struck fish with equal dexterity. For the Northern ones I can witness who several times saw them through a glass throw their Spear from 10 to 20 yards and generaly succeed; to the Southward again the plenty of Fish bones we saw near their fires provd them to be no indifferent artists.

For striking of Turtle they use a peg of wood well bearded and about a foot long: this fastens into a socket of a staff of light wood as thick as a mans wrist and 8 or 9 feet long, besides which they are tied together by a loose line of 3 or 4 fathoms in lengh. The use of this must undoubtedly be that when the Turtle is struck the staff flies off from the peg and serves for a float to shew them where the Turtle is, as well as assists to tire him till they can with their canoes overtake and haul him in. That they throw this Dart with great force we had occasion to observe while we lay in Endeavours river, where a turtle which we killd had one of them intirely buried in its body just across its breast; it seemd to have enterd at the soft place where the fore fins work but not the least outward mark of the wound remaind.

Besides these things we saw near their fire places plentifull remains of lobsters, shell fish of all kinds, and to the Southward the skins of those Sea animals which from their property of spouting out water when touchd are commonly calld sea squirts. These last, howsoever disgustfull they may seem to an European palate, we found to contain under a coat as tough as leather a substance like the guts of a shell fish, in taste tho not equal to an oyster yet by no means to be despisd by a man who is hungrey.

Of Land animals they probably eat every kind that they can kill which probably does not amount to any large number, every species being here shy and cautious in a high degree. The only vegetables we saw them use were Yams of 2 sorts, the one long and like a finger the other round and coverd with stringy roots, both sorts very small but sweet; they were so scarce where we were that we never could find the plants that producd them, tho we often saw the places where they had been dug up by the Indians very newly. It is very probable that the Dry season which was at its hight when we were there had destroyd the leaves of the plants so that we had no guides, while the Indians knowing well the stalks might find them easily. Whether they knew or ever made use of the Coccos I cannot tell; the immence sharpness of every part of this vegetable before it is dressd makes it probable that any people who have not learnd the uses of it from others may remain for ever ignorant of them. Near their fires were great abundance of the shells of a kind of fruit resembling a Pine apple very much in appearance, tho in taste disagreable enough; it is common to all the East Indies and calld by the Dutch there *Pyn appel Boomen* (*Pandanus*); as also those of the fruits of a low Palm calld by the Dutch *Moeskruidige Calappus* (*Cycas circinalis*) which they certainly eat, tho they are so unwholesome that some of our people who tho forewarnd depending upon their example eat one or 2 of were violently affected by them both upwards and downwards, and our hogs whose constitutions we thought might be as strong as those of the Indians literaly dyed after having eat them. It is probable however that these people have some method of Preparing them by which their poisonous quality is destroyd, as the inhabitants of the East Indian Isles are said to do by boiling them and steeping them 24 hours in water, then drying them and using them to thicken broth; from whence it should seem that the poisonous quality lays intirely in the Juices, as it does in the roots of the Mandihocca or Cassada of the West Indies and that when thouroughly cleard of them the pulp remaing may be a wholesome and nutritious food.

Their victuals they generaly dress by broiling or toasting them upon the coals, so we judg'd by the remains we saw; they knew however the method of baking or stewing with hot stones and sometimes practis'd it, as we now and then saw the pits and burnd stones which had been made use of for that purpose.

We observd that some tho but few held constantly in their mouths the leaves of an herb[18] which they chewd as a European does tobacca or an East Indian Betele. What sort of plant it was we had not an opportunity of learning as we never saw any thing but the chaws which they took from their

18. This was probably the plant 'pitjuri'; a tobacco-like plant with narcotic properties.

mouths to shew us; it might be of the Betele kind and so far as we could judge from the fragments was so, but whatever it was it was usd without any addition and seemd to have no kind of effect upon either the teeth or lips of those who usd it.

Naked as these people are when abroad they are scarce at all better defended from the injuries of the weather when at home, if that name can with propriety be given to their houses — as I beleive they never make any stay in them but wandering like the Arabs from place to place set them up whenever they meet with one where sufficient supplys of food are to be met with, and as soon as these are exhausted remove to another leaving the houses behind, which are framd with less art or rather less industry than any habitations of human beings probably that the world can shew.

At Sting-Rays Bay, where they were the best, each was capable of containing within it 4 or 5 people but not one of all these could in any direction extend himself his whole lengh; for hight he might just set upright, but if inclind to sleep must coil himself in some crooked position as the dimensions were in no direction long enough to hold him otherwise. They were built in the form of an oven of pliable rods about as thick as a mans finger, the Ends of which were stuck into the ground and the whole coverd with Palm leaves and broad peices of Bark; the door was a pretty large hole at one end, opposite to which by the ashes there seemd to be a fire kept pretty constantly to the Northward. Again where the warmth of the climate made houses less necessary they were in proportion still more slight; a house there was nothing but a hollow shelter about 3 or 4 feet deep built like the former and like them coverd with bark; one side of this was intirely open which was always that which was shelterd from the course of the prevailing wind, and opposite to this door was always a heap of ashes, the remains of a fire probably more necessary to defend them from Mosquetos than cold. In these it is probable that they only sought to defend their heads and the upper part of their bodies from the Draught of air, trusting their feet to the care of the fire, and so small they were that even in this manner not above 3 or 4 people could possibly croud into one of them. But small as the trouble of erecting such houses must be they did not always do it; we saw many places in the woods where they had slept with no other shelter than a few bushes and grass a foot or two high to shade them from the wind; this probably is their custom while they travel from place to place and sleep upon the road in situations where they do not mean to make any stay.

The only Furniture belonging to these houses, that we saw at least, was oblong vessels of Bark made by the simple contrivance of tying up the two ends of a longish peice with a withe[19] which not being cut off serves for a handle, these we imagind serv'd for the purpose of Water Buckets to fetch water from the springs which may sometimes be distant. We have reason to suppose that when they travel these are carried by the women from place to place; indeed the few opportunities we had of seeing the women they were generaly employd in some laborious occupation as fetching wood, gathering shell fish &c.

The men again maybe constantly carry their arms in their hands, 3 or 4 lances in one and the machine with which they throw them in the other; these serve them in the double capacity of defending them from their enemies and striking any animal or fish that they may meet with. Besides these each has a small bag about the size of a moderate Cabbage net which hangs loose upon his back fasned to a small string which passes over the crown of his head; this seems to contain all their worldly treasures, each man hardly more than might be containd in the crown of a hat — a lump or two of Paint, some fish hooks and lines, shells to make them of, Points of Darts and resin and their usual ornaments were the general contents.

Thus live these I had almost said happy people, content with little nay almost nothing, Far enough removd from the anxieties attending upon riches, or even the possession of what we Europeans call common necessaries: anxieties intended maybe by Providence to counterbalance the pleasure arising from the Posession of wishd for attainments, consequently increasing with increasing wealth, and in some measure keeping up the balance of hapiness between the rich and the

19. A cord made from plant fibres, or such things as a willow twig or a creeper.

poor. From them appear how small are the real wants of human nature, which we Europeans have increasd to an excess which would certainly appear incredible to these people could they be told it. Nor shall we cease to increase them as long as Luxuries can be invented and riches found for the purchase of them; and how soon these Luxuries degenerate into necessaries may be sufficiently evincd by the universal use of strong liquors, Tobacco, spices, Tea &c. &c. In this instance again providence seems to act the part of a leveler, doing much towards putting all ranks into an equal state of wants and consequently of real poverty: the Great and Magnificent want as much and may be more than the midling: they again in proportion more than the inferior: each rank still looking higher than his station but confining itself to a certain point above which it knows not how to wish, not knowing at least perfectly what is there enjoyd.

Tools among them we saw almost none, indeed having no arts which require any it is not to be expected that they should have many. A stone made sharp at the edge and a wooden mallet were the only ones we saw that had been formd by art; the use of these we supposd to be in making the notches in the bark of high trees by which they climb them for purposes unknown to us, and for cutting and perhaps driving wedges to take of the bark which they must have in large peices for making Canoes, Sheilds and water buckets and also for covering their houses. Besides these they use shells and corals to scrape the points of their darts, and polish them with the leaves of a kind of wild Fig tree *(Ficus Radulo)* which bites upon wood almost as keenly as our European shave grass usd by the Joiners. Their fish hooks are made of shell very neatly and some exceedingly small; their lines are also well twisted and they have them from the size of a half inch rope to almost the fineness of a hair made of some vegetable. Of Netting they seem to be quite ignorant but make their bags, the only thing of the kind we saw among them, by laying the threads loop within loop something in the way of knitting only very coarse and open, in the very same manner as I have seen ladies make purses in England. That they had no sharp instruments among them we venturd to guess from the circumstance of an old man who came to us one day with a beard rather larger than his fellows: the next day he came again, his beard was then almost croppd close to his chin and upon examination we found the ends of the hairs all burnd so that he had certainly singd it off. Their manner of Hunting and taking wild animals we had no opportunity of seeing: we only guessd that the notches which they had every where cut in the Bark of large trees, which certainly servd to make climbing more easy to them, might be intended for the ascending these trees in order either to watch for any animal who unwarily passing under them they might peirce with their darts, or for the taking birds who at night might Roost in them. We guessd also that the fires which we saw so frequently as we passd along shore, extending over a large tract of countrey and by which we could constantly trace the passage of the Indians who went from us in Endeavours river up into the countrey, were intended in some way or other for the taking of the animal calld by them *Kanguru*, which we found to be so much afraid of fire that we could hardly force it with our dogs to go over places newly burnt. They get fire very expeditiously with two peices of stick very readily and nimbly: the one must be round and 8 or nine inches long and both it and the other should be dry and soft; the round one they sharpen a little at one end and pressing it upon the other turn it round with the palms of their hands just as Europeans do a chocolate mill, often shifting their hands up and running them down quick to make the pressure as hard as possible; in this manner they will get fire in less than 2 minutes and when once posessd, of the smallest spark increase in a manner truely wonderfull. We often admird to see a man run along shore who seemd to carry no one thing in his hand and yet as he ran along, just stooping down every 50 or 100 yards, smoak and fire were seen among the drift wood and dirt at that place almost the instant he had left it. This we afterwards found was done cheifly by the infinite readyness with which every kind of rubbish, sticks, witherd leaves or dry grass already almost dryd to tinder by the heat of the sun and dryness of the season would take fire: he took for instance when he set off a small bit of fire and wrapping it up in dry grass ran on, this soon blazd, he then layd it down on the most convenient place for his purpose that he could find and taking up a small part of it wrappd that in part of the dry rubbish in which he had layd it, in this manner proceeding as long as he thought proper.

Their Weapons, offensive at least, were precisely the same where ever we saw them except that at the very last view we had of the countrey we saw through our glasses a man who carried a Bow and arrows; in this we might but I beleive we were not mistaken. They consisted of one only species, a Pike or Lance from 8 to 14 feet in lengh: this they threw short distances with their hands and for longer, 40 or more yards, with an instrument made for the purpose. The upper part of these Lances were made either of Cane or the stalk of a plant something resembling a Bullrush ([20]) which was very streight and light: the point again was made of very heavy and hard wood, the whole artfully balancd for throwing tho very clumsily made in two, three or four joints, at each of which the parts were let into each other and besides being tied round the Joint was smeard over very thick with their Resin which made it larger and more clumsey than any other part. The points were of several sorts: those which we concluded to be intended against men were indeed most cruel weapons: they were all single pointed either with the stings of sting-rays, a large one of which servd for the point, and three or 4 smaller tied the contrary way made barbs: or simply of wood made very sharp and smeard thick over with resin into which was stuck many broken bits of sharp shells, so that if such a weapon pierced a man it was many to one that it could not be drawn out without leaving several of those unwelcome guests in his flesh, certain to make the wound ten times more dificult to cure than it otherwise would be. The others which we supposd to be usd merely for striking fish, birds &c had generaly simple points of wood or if they were barbd it was with only one splinter of wood. The instrument[†] with which they threw them was a plain stick or peice of wood 2 and ½ or 3 feet in lengh, at one end of which was a small knob or hook and near the other a kind of cross peice to hinder it from slipping out of their hands. With this contrivance,

20. Banks leaves a space in the manuscript, no doubt intending to add a more precise description later.

†

simple as it is and ill fitted for the purpose, they threw the lances 40 or more yards with a swiftness and steadyness truley surprizing; the knob being hookd into a small dent made in the top of the lance they held it over their shoulder and shaking it an instant as balancing threw it with the greatest ease imaginable. The neatest of these throwing sticks that we saw were made of a hard reddish wood polish and shining; their sides were flat and about 2 inches in breadth and the handle or part to keep it from dropping out of the hand coverd with thin layers of polished bone very white; these I beleive to be the things which many of our people were deceivd by imagining them to be wooden swords, Clubs &c. according to the direction in which they happned to see them. Defensive weapons we saw only in Sting-Rays bay and there only a single instance — a man who attempted to oppose our Landing came down to the Beach with a sheild of an oblong shape about 3 feet long and 1½ broad made of the bark of a tree; this he left behind when he ran away and we found upon taking it up that it plainly had been piercd through with a single pointed lance near the center. That such sheilds were frequently usd in that neighbourhood we had however sufficient proof, often seeing upon trees the places from whence they had been cut and sometimes the sheilds themselves cut out but not yet taken off from the tree; the edges of the bark only being a little raisd with wedges; which shews that these people certainly know how much thicker and stronger bark becomes by being sufferd to remain upon the tree some time after it is cut round.

That they are a very pusilanimous people we had reason to suppose from every part of their conduct in every place where we were except Sting Rays bay, and there only the instance of the two people who opposd the Landing of our two boats full of men for near a quarter of an hour and were not to be drove away till serveral times wounded with small shot, which we were obligd to do as at that time we suspected their Lances to be poisned from the quantity of gum which was about their points; but upon every other occasion both there and every where else they behavd alike, shunning us and giving up any part of the countrey which we landed upon at once: and that they use stratagems in war we learnt by the instance in Sting-rays bay where our Surgeon with another man walking in the woods met 8 Indians; they stood still but directed another who was up in a tree how and when he should throw a Lance at them, which he did and on its not taking effect they all ran away as fast as possible.

Their Canoes were the only things in which we saw a manifest difference between the Southern and Northern people. Those to the Southward were little better contrivd or executed than their Houses: a peice of Bark tied together in Pleats at the ends and kept extended in the middle by small bows of wood was the whole embarkation, which carried one or two, nay we once saw three people, who movd it along in shallow water by setting with long poles; and in deeper by padling with padles about 18 inches long, one of which they held in each hand. In the middle of these Canoes was generaly a small fire upon a heap of sea weed, for what purpose intended we did not learn except perhaps to give the fisherman an opportunity of Eating fish in perfection by broiling it the moment it is taken.

To the Northward again their canoes tho exceeding bad were far superior to these. They were small but regularly hollowd out of the trunk of a tree and fitted with an outrigger to prevent them from oversetting; in these they had paddles large enough to require both hands to work them. Of this sort we saw only   [21] and had an opportunity of examining only one of them which might be about 10 or 11 feet long but was immensely narrow; the sides of the tree were left in their natural state untouch'd by tools but at each [end] they had cut off from the under part and left part of the upper side overhanging; the inside also was not ill hollowd and the sides tolerably thin. What burthen it was capable of carrying we had many times an opportunity to see: 3 people or at most 4 were as many as dare venture in it and if any more wanted to come over the river, which in that place was about a half a mile broad, one of these would carry back the Canoe and fetch them.

21. Space left by Banks in the manuscript.

This was the only peice of workmanship which I saw among the New Hollanders that seemd to require tools. How they had hollowd her out or cut the ends I cannot guess but upon the whole the work was not ill done; Indian patience might do a great deal with shells &c. without the use of stone axes, which if they had had they would propably have used to form her outside as well as inside. That such a canoe takes them up much time and trouble in the making may be concluded from our seeing so few, and still more from the moral certainty which we have that the Tribe which visited [us] and consisted to our knowledge of 21 people and may be of several more had only one such belonging to them. How tedious must it be for these people to be ferried over a river a mile or two wide by threes and fours at a time: how well therefore worth the pains for them to stock themselves better with boats if they could do it!

I am inclind to beleive that besides these Canoes the Northern People know and make use of the Bark one of the South, and that from having seen one of the small paddles left by them upon a small Island where they had been fishing for Turtle; it lay upon a heap of Turtle shells and bones, Trophies of the good living they had had when there, and with it lay a broken staff of a Turtle pegg and a rotten line, tools which had been worn out I suppose in the service of Catching them. We had great reason to beleive that at some season of the year the weather is much more moderate than we found it, otherwise the Indians never could have venturd in any canoes that we saw half so far from the main Land as Islands were on which we saw evident marks of their having been, such as decayd houses, fires, the before mentiond Turtle bones &c. May be at this more moderate time they may make and use such Canoes, and when the Blustering season comes on may convert the bark of which they were made to the purposes of covering houses, making Water buckets &c. &c. well knowing that when the next season returns they will not want a supply of bark to rebuild their vessels. Another reason we have to imagine that such a moderate season exists, and that the Winds are then upon the Eastern board as we found them, is that whatever Indian houses or sleeping places we saw on these Islands were built upon the summits of small hills if there were any, or if not, in places where no bushes or wood could intercept the course of the wind, and their shelter was always turnd to the

Eastward. On the main again, their houses were universaly built in valleys, or under the shelter of trees which might defend them from the very winds which in the Islands they exposd themselves to.

Of their Language I can say very little. Our acquaintance with them was of so short a duration that none of us attempted to use a single word of it to them, consequently the list of words I have given could be got no other manner than by signs enquiring of them what in their Language signified such a thing, a method obnoxious to many mistakes: for instance a man holds in his hand a stone and asks the name of [it]: the Indian may return him for answer either the real name of a stone, one of the properties of it as hardness, roughness, smoothness &c, one of its uses or the name peculiar to some particular species of stone, which name the enquirer immediately sets down as that of a stone. To avoid however as much as Possible this inconvenience Myself and 2 or 3 more got from them as many words as we could, and having noted down those which we though[t] from circumstances we were not mistaken in we compard our lists; those in which all the lists agreed, or rather were contradicted by none, we thought our selves moraly certain not to be mistaken in. Of these my list cheefly consists, some only being added that were in only one list such as from the ease with which signs might be contrivd to ask them were thought little less certain than the others.

Wageegee	the head	*Meanang*	Fire
Morye	the hair	*Walba*	a stone
Melcea	the ears	*Yowall*	Sand
Yembe	the Lips	*Gurka*	a Rope
Bonjoo	the Nose	*Bama*	a Man
Unjar	the tongue	*Poinja*	a male Turtle
Wallar	the Beard	*Mameingo*	a female
Doomboo	the Neck	*Maragan*	a Canoe
Cayo	the Nipples	*Pelenyo*	to Paddle
Toolpoor	the Navel	*Takai*	Set down
Mangal	the Hands	*Mierbarrar*	smooth
Coman	the thighs	*Garmbe*	Blood
Pongo	the Knees	*Yocou*	Wood
Edamal	the Feet	*Tapool*	bone in nose
Kniorror	the Heel	*Charngala*	a Bag

Chumal	the Sole	*Cherr*	} expressions maybe of
Chongarn	the ancle	*Cherco*	} admiration which they
Kulk	the Nails	*Yarcaw*	} continualy usd while
Gallan	the Sun	*Tut tut tut tut*	} in company with us

They very often use the article *Ge* which seems to answer to our English 'a' as *Ge Gurka* a rope.

Sources of illustrations

All illustrations are from the collection of the Mitchell Library, State Library of New South Wales, unless otherwise stated.

1. Sir Joseph Banks. Mezzotint by W. Dickinson after Sir Joshua Reynolds, 1774. ML P3/37
2. *National Geographic* magazine
3. "Chart of the South Pacifick Ocean, pointing out the discoveries made therin previous to 1764", in Alexander Dalrymple, *An account of the discoveries made in the South Pacifick Ocean, previous to 1764*, London, 1767. ML 980/103A1
4. "Flying Fish of St Jago – Cape De Verde Island", George Tobin Sketches on HMS *Providence*, 1791. ML ZPXA 563 f5
5. "Portuguese Man of War (So Called by Seamen)", George Tobin Sketches on HMS *Providence*, 1791. ML ZPXA 563 f5
6. "Botany Bay, in New South Wales . . .", in John Hawkesworth, *An account of the voyages undertaken by order of His Present Majesty for making discoveries in the Southern Hemisphere,* Vol 3. London, 1773. ML Q980/38A3
7. "Banksia Serrata" in *Banks' Florilegium*, London, Alecto Historical Editions in association with British Museum (Natural History), 1981–1988. ML XX/84
8. "Acacia" in *Banks' Florilegium,* London, Alecto Historical Editions in association with the British Museum (Natural History), 1981–1988. ML XX/84
9. Sydney Parkinson in Sydney Parkinson, *A journal of a voyage to the South Seas,* London, 1773. ML Q980/P
10. Mount Warning, in John Hawkesworth, *An account of the voyages undertaken by order of His Present Majesty for making discoveries in the Southern Hemisphere,* Vol 3. London, 1773. ML Q980/38A3
11. "Xylomelum", in *Banks' Florilegium,* London, Alecto Historical Editions in association with the British Museum (Natural History), 1981–1988. ML XX/84

12. "The Kanguroo, an Animal found on the coast of New Holland" [detail], in John Hawkesworth, *An account of the voyages undertaken by order of His Present Majesty for making discoveries in the Southern Hemisphere*, Vol 3. London, 1773. ML Q980/38A3

13. "Two of the Natives of New Holland, Advancing to Combat", in Sydney Parkinson, *A journal of a voyage to the South Seas*, London, 1773. ML Q980/P

14. "A view of Endeavour River, on the Coast of New Holland where the ship was laid ashore to repair the damage she received on the rock", in Sydney Parkinson, *A journal of a voyage to the South Seas,* London, 1773. ML Q980/P

15. "Entrance of Endeavour River in New South Wales . . .", in John Hawkesworth, *An account of the voyages undertaken by order of His Present Majesty for making discoveries in the Southern Hemisphere,* Vol 3. London, 1773. ML Q980/38A3

16. "Dendrobium" in *Banks' Florilegium,* London, Alecto Historical Editions in association with the British Museum (Natural History), 1981–1988. ML XX/84

17. "Bonetta", George Tobin Sketches on HMS *Providence,* 1791. ML ZPX A 563 f10

18. Dr James Stuart. Untitled [Blue Swimmer Crab], 1841. ML PXD 133 f73

19. "A Chart of New South Wales or the East Coast of New Holland . . .", in John Hawkesworth, *An account of the voyages undertaken by order of His Present Majesty for making discoveries in the Southern Hemisphere,* Vol 3. London, 1773. ML Q980/38A3

20. "Chart of Part of the South Sea Shewing the Tracts and Discoveries made by . . . Endeavour . . .", in John Hawkesworth, *An account of the voyages undertaken by order of His Present Majesty for making discoveries in the Southern Hemisphere,* Vol 3. London, 1773. ML Q980/38A3

21. Thomas Phillips. Sir Joseph Banks oil c1809. ML DG25